KU-034-458

J. R. HARTLEY
CASTS AGAIN

J. R. HARTLEY
CASTS AGAIN

More Memories of
Angling Days

ILLUSTRATED BY
PATRICK BENSON

Stanley Paul

LONDON SYDNEY AUCKLAND
JOHANNESBURG

Stanley Paul & Co Ltd

An imprint of Random House (UK) Limited
20 Vauxhall Bridge Road, London SW1V 2SA

Random House Australia (Pty) Ltd
20 Alfred Street, Milsons Point, Sydney 2061

Random House New Zealand Limited
18 Poland Road, Glenfield, Auckland 10

Random House South Africa (Pty) Ltd
PO Box 337, Bergvlei 2012, South Africa

First published 1992

Copyright © Michael Russell (Publishing) Ltd 1992

The right of J. R. Hartley to be identified as the author of this
work has been asserted by him in accordance with the
Copyright, Designs and Patents Act, 1988

'Yellow Pages' and the 'Walking Fingers' logos
are registered trademarks of
British Telecommunications plc in the UK

Set in Sabon by The Typesetting Bureau, Wimborne, Dorset
Printed and bound in Great Britain
by Butler and Tanner Ltd, Frome, Somerset

A catalogue record for this book is available
upon request from the British Library

ISBN 0 09 177437 3

Contents

Acknowledgements

To Yellow Pages for projecting me; to ace fisherman Peter Lapsley for advising me; to Michael Russell for writing me; to Patrick Benson for illustrating me; to Roderick Bloomfield for publishing me.

J.R.H.

I

A Flying Visit

I always liked my wife's Uncle Reggie. He was a real goer: fearless, amusing and usually misdirected, a stylish fly fisherman and an appalling driver – one of the few motorists alive to have derailed a train. He became known in the family as 'The Swerver' because of his inventive opportunism and his capacity to accelerate away from trouble – which tended to be economic, if only because there was no room in Uncle Reggie's life plan for employment. He acquired over the years a huge store of haphazard information, which he imparted with such enthusiasm and conviction that it was always tempting to believe what he said, although probably no more than half of it was true.

He had inherited the Wilkeses' family home in North Norfolk, a Georgian twelve-bedroomed house called Pitremington Hall. It looked over a rather unkempt small park of about thirty acres, adapting gradually to compromised standards of repair. There had been a couple of gravel pits in the palmier days to support Uncle Reggie's life style, but they expired in due season and left him to live on his wits. In a reckless moment he bought two London properties during the blitz, which miraculously evaded damage and which he sold in the early 1950s for a massive profit.

Pitremington Hall mouldered uncomplainingly away as Uncle Reggie pursued his frantic life of economic snakes and ladders. The remains of the London property profits went on a venture into bloodstock and by the time the last yearling was pronounced useless, most of the top-floor bedrooms at the Hall had buckets on the floor to catch the rain. It was a time for imaginative decision; but that was Uncle Reggie's forte. He managed to cajole four aging gentlefolk into taking up residence in exchange for generous commitments of capital. Pitremington Hall was given a comprehensive facelift and Uncle Reggie a new lease of financial life.

The residents all came rather into the category of 'reduced to clear'. First there was Lady Senlac, a Colonial Service widow beached on a strand of imperial memories. Then there was Major Dillamore, late of the Indian Army, who spent most of his time reading the financial press and punting on the Stock Exchange. Next there was Hedley Mearns, a near-extinguished flame with a very soft voice and exquisite manners. And finally Malcolm Spenniford, a deranged cigar importer who had bouts of imagining he was Louis Blériot and ran through the reception rooms pretending to be an aeroplane. To cope with these profitable nestlings Uncle Reggie engaged a housekeeper-cum-troubleshooter called Miss Palmer, who was very fond of cats. Pitremington Hall recovered its bloom and Uncle Reggie, with his hand on the financial tiller, had the well-satisfied look of a round-the-world sailor heading safely into port.

Uncle Reggie had fishing on the River Babingley, a delightful little chalk stream, no more than eight or nine miles long, that rises as a number of tiny brooks which bubble up from springs in the meadows between Flitcham and Hillington. The brooks join before running into the lake at Hillington Hall, where further springs give the river that extra body to skirt the eastern boundary of the Sandringham Estate, nose on past Castle Rising and lose itself in The Wash ten miles east of King's Lynn. It is probably only about twenty feet wide at its widest, with rather ill-kempt banks – at least on Uncle Reggie's water – and a chiefly gravel bed, though lower down, beyond the A149, there are some silted stretches. The brown trout run fairly routinely up to two pounds, but two and a half to three would be a whopper.

Lawrence Wilkes, my brother-in-law, and my wife Helen and I had been invited by Uncle Reggie to try our luck on the Babingley one June weekend. Lawrence at that time was very keen on flying and with the support of the Yeovil Flying Club had recently obtained a pilot's licence. He decided therefore that he and Helen would fly up to Norfolk on the Saturday morning in a Tiger Moth, while I went up on the Friday in the car. The plan was full of anxiety in whatever combination it was presented, but Lawrence was confident and probably Helen secretly considered her brother and the Tiger Moth a better bet than myself and the Morris Oxford, even if I could expect to travel at safer altitudes.

It was past eleven o'clock on Friday evening when I turned into the drive and headed up towards the house. There were quite a few lights still on and when I opened the front door and came into the hall I saw Uncle Reggie and Miss Palmer bent over a ping-pong table, on which they had spread out a very large jigsaw puzzle. Uncle Reggie was expansively welcoming. He asked about my journey and said 'Let's get in your things', although, when it came to it, this invitation appeared not to include himself. When Miss Palmer and I returned with the luggage he gestured towards a tray of sandwiches and a bottle of red wine, and while continuing to concentrate on the jigsaw began to tell me about the medical progress that had been made in the combating of Bell's palsy. Coming from most people this could have seemed a less than run-of-the-mill topic, but being familiar with the broadness of Uncle Reggie's conversational brush I refused to be surprised and listened attentively as I ate my sandwiches. I had contributed no more than a few 'Really?'s and one 'Goodness me', when we were interrupted by the appearance on the stairs of Lady Senlac in battened-down hair and a blue dressing gown.

'Miss Palmer,' she said in an accusing voice, 'there's a Humboldt's spider in the bath.'

'A what?' said Uncle Reggie, squinting at two indistinguishable pieces of jigsaw.

'A Humboldt's spider,' Lady Senlac repeated. 'We used to get them in the Sudan. I've seen lots.'

'So had Lot's wife,' said Uncle Reggie, 'and look what happened to her.'

I thought this a bit steep for mixed company, and I was relieved to see that Lady Senlac hadn't quite measured up to the full implications, since she was fortunately distracted by Miss Palmer's materialising with some counter-spider equipment and joining her on the stairs. As they went up together to relocate the intruder we heard Lady Senlac explaining to Miss Palmer that they 'came in on the boats'.

Uncle Reggie shook his head. 'Just imagine,' he said, 'coming all the way from Africa on some frightful tramp steamer, walking half way across East Anglia, shinning up the inside of a waste pipe, struggling out of the plughole, and the first thing you see is Amy Senlac in her dressing gown looking like a plate of malevolent brandysnaps.'

He was right. But trust Uncle Reggie to take the spider's side.

The morning news from Miss Palmer was that Lawrence and Helen were expecting to arrive shortly after lunch in the Tiger Moth and that Lawrence proposed to land in the park. I had come down to breakfast a shade before Uncle Reggie and I was rather self-consciously down-table from

Lady Senlac, who was eating a piece of toast with small, purposeful mouthfuls, her hair back in day order, and apparently none the worse for her encounter with the spider. I was a little flustered as to whether my having seen her in her night rig constituted an admissable sighting or whether it would be more decorous to pretend our acquaintance was starting from scratch; so, deciding in favour of the latter, I introduced myself as J. R. Hartley and said I was a fishing friend of Uncle Reggie. Lady Senlac acknowledged this information with a gracious smile, picked up *The Times* and turned to the Court Circular.

Uncle Reggie arrived in a clatter. He smacked the back of Lady Senlac's paper with his open palm.

'Keeping up with the Joneses, Amy?' he boomed, alluding to her interest in social affairs.

'I don't think I know the Joneses,' Lady Senlac replied evenly, straightening out her paper without complaint as though Uncle Reggie were some miscreant but favourite dog.

I watched with curiosity. The good-humoured distance between them, I came to the conclusion, was in fact a form of closeness. It said much for Uncle Reggie's charm that he could find sap in sticks like Lady Senlac.

I told him about Lawrence's plans, and soon our conversation turned to our morning on the river. There should be Pale Wateries, he said, hatching around midday, and he'd expect to see some Iron Blue Duns and Blue-Winged Olives about. He recommended that I fish an Iron Blue, an Orange Quill or a Little Marryat during the first session. Later, when Lawrence and Helen joined us for the evening rise, it might pay to try a Sherry Spinner, or perhaps a Cinnamon Sedge.

We were interrupted by a loud sputtering sound and a man ran into the room with his arms outstretched, apparently simulating the flight of an aeroplane. He wore goggles and a hat like an oversized beret. He came into land on the chair opposite Lady Senlac, who wished him a polite good morning and told him there were some sausages on the sideboard. At this he took off again with a tremendous revving noise, downing one wing to get a grip on the serving spoon.

'Malcolm Spenniford,' Uncle Reggie said, more in explanation than introduction. 'No, I mean Louis Blériot.'

The aeronaut bowed.

'Bonjour,' I said. 'Have you yet flown the Channel?'

He pushed up his goggles. 'Perhaps today,' he said.

Uncle Reggie shielded one side of his face with a hand and mouthed 'Harmless.'

I hoped so.

Uncle Reggie was mouthing again. 'Attention-seeking.'

Likely to succeed.

Only Uncle Reggie, I reflected, could be sitting here on even terms with a raver and a rolling pin, having coaxed away the bulk of their life savings for the refurbishment of his house. The arrival, over the next few minutes, of the rest of Uncle Reggie's human portfolio expanded my admiration even more.

Major Dillamore, flicking from page to page of the financial press and pausing now and then to write something down in a notebook, kept saying to himself 'Interesting.' This must have been what he supposed was the unlocking of some crucial company secret, but the most interesting thing about Major Dillamore's playing of the stock market was that he never made any money.

Hedley Mearns took ages to spread butter on his toast and gave genial little smiles to everyone without actually saying anything. He was impeccably dressed and groomed, with not a hair out of place. He was about the most pleasantly ineffective man you could ever meet, a sort of human meringue. Like the rest of the household he seemed devoted to Uncle Reggie.

We got up to leave the table.

'Goodbye, Amy,' Uncle Reggie said to Lady Senlac, 'be kind to the natives.'

She made the merest concession to a smile. 'I shall, Reggie.'

Uncle Reggie turned to the aeronaut.

'Cheerio, Blériot,' he said, making the two words rhyme in an unnecessarily philistine way. Then he waved a hand to Hedley Mearns, wished the Major tight lines and followed me out of the room.

I asked him about the aeronaut as we walked out to survey the weather from the front steps.

'Has he always been like that?'

'No,' said Uncle Reggie. 'In the days when he had his cigar business he seemed reasonably normal. When he said he'd come in with me, obviously I realised he was slightly batty. It never occurred to me he'd turn into a French aviator.'

'What does the doctor say?'

'Dr Halpin? He looked him over and thought he was safe. He said he'd keep an eye on him, but as one of his eyes is glass it rather matters which one.'

'I see,' I said. I had the feeling that Uncle Reggie was taking the matter too lightly. His come-uppance and Monsieur Blériot's come-downance might be one and the same thing; and, from what I'd just seen, imminent. He interrupted my reflections to suggest that we go in his car. It wasn't much of a prospect but I tried to sound pleased.

I'd brought an eight-foot-six split-cane rod – not the one that my father had bought me all those years ago from the major in Wotton-under-Edge, with a splice in it where it got caught in the front wheel of my bicycle, but a newer one, with a splice in it where Helen had broken it trying to dislodge a walnut that our daughter had pushed up the Morris's exhaust. I still used a silk line (the plastic lines hadn't quite come in at that stage), a canvas fishing bag with leather straps, and a hooped cane landing net with a cane handle and a heavy knotted mesh. When you caught a fish you washed the fly in the stream and then dried it by squeezing it in a pad of dried amadou – a thin sheet cut from the amadou fungus, a bracket fungus which grows on trees, especially on the silver birches that abound on that sandy North Norfolk terrain.

There was not much traffic about, which was just as well because Uncle Reggie tended to be possessive about the crown of the road. He also had that unwelcome habit of turning to talk to you while he was driving and it seemed uncivil to suggest that he should look where he was going. Still, the sun was in the heavens, the hedgerows were white with elder and spotted pink with dog roses, there was freshness in the colours of the countryside – and we were going fishing.

We parked the car in a gateway and walked down through a rough meadow deliciously slovenly with white-flowered meadowsweet and purple bog orchids. There is always an excitement in your first glimpse of new water, you look at it rather in the manner of the bishop who always found himself wondering, as he went up a cathedral aisle, whether it would take spin.

I was wearing thigh waders. I parted the bankside growth cautiously, with Uncle Reggie at my elbow. The water was clear, with quite reasonable movement to keep the weed pliant, and there was watercress along the river's margins. Almost at once I saw a fish rise on the far side, and I turned to Uncle Reggie. He had seen it too. He nodded for me to go ahead and quietly – well, fairly quietly – withdrew back into the meadow, where he watched for a few moments before moving off downstream.

I missed that first fish and soon I was beginning to wonder if I had misread the day. Then, around noon, a really good rise began – first those odd movements, like the first bold spots of a storm, then a flicker of little fellows and here and there something much more solid: substance as well as confidence.

There are not many experienced anglers who have been spared the frustration of being temporarily immobilised when everything is so inviting and when you know the rise can die away as quickly as it began. I caught two fish of about a pound and a half each, and then I had trouble with my reel and had to clamber back on to the bank for hasty repairs with the little screwdriver that always travelled with me in the fishing bag.

My pit stop over, I prepared to wade out into the river again, reassured to see that there was still movement up and down the water. Then I noticed with mixed feelings that Uncle Reggie was coming up the bank towards me. He raised his landing net, partly in greeting, partly to show me two good brown trout curved in the mesh. Then he called out, from perhaps twenty yards away, 'I'll tell you something very interesting. Do you know one of the principal reasons why we won those early battles against the French?'

I did, as it happened, have views on the subject, but they weren't going to repulse Uncle Reggie's. I extended the line with my left hand and made a few steps into the vegetation on the river's edge. Uncle Reggie closed on me. There was an awful relentlessness about him in his informative moods.

'It was the way the longbowmen were taught to use their bows. The French extended the left arm and pulled back the right, while the English kept their left arms bent as they pulled back the right. Then, at the last moment, they leant into the bow with an extended left arm and the arrow carried that much further.'

No one welcomes a historical nugget more than I, even if the informant is as suspect as Uncle Reggie; but not, please, when the brownies are on the boil and I've just lost four precious minutes repairing my reel. And although confirmation of our natural supremacy over the French is welcome at any time, there will be moments when my frisson of pleasure is on minimum throb. This was one of them.

'Just lend me your rod a minute,' Uncle Reggie said, 'and I'll show you what I mean.'

I passed him the rod. He wound the line four or five times round it near the point, attached my Little Marryat to the reel, gripped the rod in the middle, extended the line with his right hand, then thrust his left arm forward with a loud grunt. It may have won the Battle of Agincourt but it broke my beloved split cane eight inches above the handle. We both stared in dismay.

'So much for patriotism,' said Uncle Reggie. 'I'm very, very sorry; but I think we can get it spliced.' He took the rod in both hands and rubbed the top section with his thumb. 'I see you've spliced it once already.'

'Yes,' I said. 'That was after the Battle of Crécy.'

We came back past Castle Rising, which used to be a 'significant little port', Uncle Reggie shouted above the noise of the car engine which he was driving in an inappropriate gear. The port apparently went into decline when ships became too large to navigate the Babingley. I guessed, correctly, that the sight of that huge Norman keep would remind Uncle Reggie that Queen Isabella was quartered there following her complicity in that deeply unmotherly action involving Edward II and the red-hot poker. Uncle Reggie asked me how long I thought I should survive with a poker so positioned, which I knew was not long, but being by nature very squeamish preferred not to consider too precisely. Uncle Reggie, unstoppable when he had the historical bit between his teeth, became so unsavoury that, at risk of appearing a back seat driver, I distracted him by pointing out that for the past mile or so a fire engine had been on our tail. At this he consulted the driving mirror and confirmed that indeed the fire engine was trying to overtake.

'Better let him past,' he called out, wrenching the car across to bump along the verge. As the engine stormed by, he rejoined the road and set off in pursuit. We gradually closed on the appliance, in the face of some fairly hostile gesticulation from the crew. Uncle Reggie, with the accelerator pressed against the floor, merely waved back good-naturedly, as if in deliberate misinterpretation of their mood. At every junction I prayed that our routes would part company, but to no avail. When at the final point of possible reprieve the fire engine took the road to Pitremington, it became apparent that this insane procession must continue all the way home. The chase, however, took on quite a new dimension when, on reaching the gates of the Hall, the fire engine swung sharply right and led us up the drive, coming to a slithering halt on the gravel sweep in front of the house, with ourselves in close attendance.

There was no evidence of fire. Miss Palmer was standing on the front steps, peering up above her. Our eyes followed the direction of her attention. On a flat section of the roof, some forty feet above, M. Blériot was crouching with arms outstretched, making little backward and forward hops as if to simulate an aircraft straining at the chocks. It looked as if this was after all cross-Channel day and a serious accident was imminent.

You didn't have to be in the shakeup for a Nobel Prize to predict that the aeronaut's flightpath was likely to be of almost vertical descent and that, given the customary acceleration factor of 22 feet per second squared, the most useful apparatus around the touchdown point was likely to be a brush and dustpan. Admittedly the wind direction was directly in his favour, but as it was no more than, in Beaufort's Scale terms, a 'light air', it couldn't reasonably be expected to add more than an infinitesimal smidgen to the flight period. No, any muggins could have calculated the probable point of impact to within a couple of feet.

It was a surprise therefore that the blanket party was sited at least twenty-five yards to the left, around a garden seat which stood against the front of the house. The fact that Lady Senlac was actually seated, with one gloved hand holding her corner of the blanket over her knees, made me wonder if considerations of personal comfort had been allowed to get the better of aspirations for M. Blériot's survival. The other three members of the posse – Major Dillamore, Mr Mearns and Eric the gardener – had also adopted an extremely half-hearted stance at their respective corners of the blanket.

Uncle Reggie, distinctly rattled, took control. He turned to me, still gripping the steering wheel. 'Get up there and keep him talking. I'll get the firemen to give him an upward squirt if he jumps.'

The idea of M. Blériot maintaining altitude in the manner of a ping-pong ball in a shooting range seemed fanciful, and I doubted if Uncle Reggie's suggestion could hope for endorsement from the brigade. I hesitated only to snatch my fishing net out of the back of the car and then I was following Miss Palmer into the house and up the stairs.

I have not much head for heights and it must have been the impetus of Uncle Reggie's personality that shot me up a ladder in one of the attics and out through the skylight on to the roof. I skirted a chimney stack, trying not to look below me, and found myself halfway down the broad lead valley which our aeronaut had selected for his runway.

At the sight of me, M. Blériot jumped excitedly up and down and shivered his wings.

'If you could hold on a few minutes,' I called, in that emphasis-English I tend to use when addressing people of other nationalities, 'my brother-in-law will be landing here in his Tiger Moth and will be very honoured to meet you.'

M. Blériot looked at me suspiciously. 'History awaits me,' he replied.

I decided not to tell him that history was in for a very short wait if he opted for takeoff before either the fire ladder appeared or Lady Senlac's outfielders could be substantially repositioned. I remembered Uncle Reggie's instructions. Keep him talking.

'My brother-in-law wanted you to show him some of your stunts. He's one of your greatest admirers.'

'I can wait only two minutes,' M. Blériot decided.

Please let there be a miracle. I strained my ears for the faintest hum of the approaching Tiger Moth. The seconds dragged by as I larded the aeronaut with compliments. They sounded a little hollow.

I could tell I hadn't won his confidence.

'What are you doing with that net?' he asked.

'The net? We've just been fishing and I rushed straight up to see you take off. I'd have had my rod too, but Reggie broke it.'

'Throw it away,' M. Blériot ordered.

'If I throw it down, will you wait just three minutes more to see if the Tiger Moth arrives?'

M. Blériot considered the proposition. He nodded.

'O.K.'

I edged slowly towards the edge of the roof. Looking back over my shoulder, I saw Miss Palmer's face at the skylight, transmitting some indeterminable newsflash. She pointed towards the end of the runway and raised her thumb in an optimistic gesture.

Almost at once I heard a grind and a bump and up above the level of the roof the fire brigade's ladder appeared, followed almost immediately by a helmet and then a rubicund face. I looked hastily round to see what effect this development might be having on the history-maker.

He seemed deranged, incensed that he was being tricked.

'Come down, Biggles,' the fireman shouted.

It was the last straw. The aeronaut pulled down his goggles

and, with wings extended and a crescendo of engine noise, swept into his takeoff.

'Wait, wait,' I screamed. Then, as he accelerated past me, I brought my landing net down over his head. His groundspeed was such that it wrested the net out of my hands, but he fell backwards, shot along the lead valley with his legs extended in front of him and struck into the fireladder, cueing both ladder and fireman back into the void.

Ground control soon brought them back heavily against the gutter, sending a section of it crashing down between Lady Senlac's party and the front steps. The fireman clambered onto the roof and tipped back his helmet.

'He's mad,' he said about the winded aeronaut.

It was hard to dispute. We helped the fallen Icarus to his feet. The spirit seemed gone out of him as he limped back with us towards the skylight. Then, unmistakably, we heard the sound of an aero engine and there, to the south, was the Tiger Moth. We stood together in silence as the plane, bobbing and quivering, came in perilously close above the trees, banked steeply and, with an unnerving bounce, landed on the drive. The fire brigade applauded.

'Come on,' I said to M. Blériot.

We all went downstairs and out of the front door. Lawrence and Helen had got out of the Tiger Moth and were standing talking to Uncle Reggie. They turned as I emerged with the fireman and the dejected aeronaut. I wanted to introduce him to Lawrence and Helen, but I sensed the matter was in other hands. Dr Halpin stepped forward and took him by the arm. I was sad. I hate to see a man so humbled.

'What happened to poor old Blériot?' I asked Uncle Reggie on the telephone a few weeks later.

'Don't talk to me about that bastard,' he replied tersely. 'I had to pay him back his money and they put him into a home. He thinks he's St Francis of Assisi, and he just sits there in a brown dressing gown waving to song thrushes out of the window.'

'I hope they don't give him ideas about flying,' I said.

2

Patents Pending

We had a plan for part of August. Uncle Reggie had suggested it, and a prerequisite of any plan of Uncle Reggie's was that it should kill at least two birds with one stone – preferably a whole aviary. This was one of Uncle Reggie's better plans.

He was very good with children, probably because he hadn't entirely grown up himself. His material trappings gave him a certain authority, yes, but he had no personal *gravitas*; and this appealed to children, even if most adults found it a shortcoming. My daughter Barbara, for instance, adored him, and he her. Towards the end of the Fifties he began to take her sailing in the little boat he kept at Brancaster and otherwise indulged her to a point almost beyond repair. So part of the summer had to be allocated to a visit to Pitremington Hall.

Helen liked sailing; I didn't, it made me nervous. Being driven on land by Uncle Reggie was quite bad enough, but at least when you hit something you didn't drown. So this August Helen and Barbara would stay in Norfolk while my brother-in-law Lawrence and I went for some free fishing organised by Uncle Reggie on condition that we tested his inventions. The location was to be the River Esk in

Cumberland, as it was called before these latter days of Cumbria.

We all drove up to Norfolk together and Lawrence and I stayed on a day for Uncle Reggie to brief us on the inventions. He said that we all knew as fishermen what the problems were. All you had to do was use your imagination and come up with a few practical suggestions. (This, before you start getting ideas, is an over-simplification.) He ended his preamble by declaring that necessity was the mother of invention. Lawrence and I agreed with him. Privately, we had doubts about Uncle Reggie being the father.

The Cementigrip Suction Waders, for instance; or the Armsplint Night Rod; the Kneepad Lunch Box; the Forage Cap Pencil Torch; the Rotatocard Pop-Up Fly Dispenser; the Lay Priest Bolt Gun; the swordfish-resistant Walnut Floataway Jacket; or, *pièce de résistance*, the Puffemoff Midge Repellent Apparatus, with cardboard-burning back-pack incinerator, back-knee bellows, and Crown of Thorns smoke dissemination head unit; and so on. We looked at them in amused bewilderment. Beekeepers or the Ministry of Defence looked a more likely market than the ordinary tackle shop, but we listened dutifully and promised to list the pros and cons. Uncle Reggie stressed that he'd chosen the Esk because it was primarily night fishing for sea trout at this time of the year. And night fishing problems were day fishing problems compounded. Which seemed another way of saying that night fishing is day fishing in the dark.

The Esk rises high on Borrowdale Fells in the Cumbrian mountains, between Ullscarf and High White Stones, then flows south-westwards between Scafell Pike and Bow Fell, before turning westwards into Eskdale. After Boot, where it is reinforced by Whillan Beck, it runs past Beckfoot and Muncaster Castle to find the sea at Ravenglass. This is quite austere country, the fells steep and bleak, the valleys hardly bountiful, with patches of woodland and fields bordered by dry stone walls. The villages are scattered, with houses of dark grey stone and roofed with slate. But there is a stern, uncompromising beauty about it all, the beauty of scale and silence under the slow play of changing light.

We were bound for the excellent Mrs Marsden, a farmer's widow who took in paying guests. She had a solid whitewashed farmhouse planted on a bare slope perhaps four or five miles from the foot of the dale, with a short path down to the single-track road and the merest concession to horticulture at the back. At this time of the year it was mostly fishermen, she said, but some people came to walk and she'd even had a writer, though he didn't seem to do much writing.

A Welsh collie called Sprat watched us cautiously from under the kitchen table as Mrs Marsden made us welcome. She asked us whether we knew these parts and we both said no. Oh, she said, well, it was an experience for us. Yes, we said, and we were sure it was going to be a most enjoyable one.

She was a little isolated, she told us, but not really lonely. People were so friendly round about and they kept in touch, particularly since her Ted was called. We felt we should ask about Ted and the circumstances of his summons, so we heard how he'd had this bump come up on his side and three months later they'd taken him away thin as a ghost. It wasn't a jolly topic but she invested it with such an un-sorrowful and matter-of-fact delivery and followed it so closely with an inquiry as to what we'd like with our scones that any expression of sympathy seemed out of place. No, she didn't know Norfolk, she said, as she filled the teapot, she'd been to Hull, and her granny, one of her grannies, came from Galashiels, that was over the Border, but Norfolk, no; it must have been quite a run, one side to the other? Yes, we said, we'd be glad to sit down to the scones.

We got on to fishing. Most of her angling people went fishing at night, she said, when the sea trout came up, plenty of small fish, just occasionally a whopper. One of the gentlemen last year caught a ten-pounder and she'd cooked it up for them and had some herself. 'We loved it, didn't we, Sprat?' she said to the dog, which slapped its tail in agreement on the flagstone floor.

She showed us our rooms, everything tidy, nothing forgotten. From my window I could see the river down below, between the trees, a series of long, slow, deep pools – they call them 'dubs' up there – connected by babbling stickles, and here and there a patch of shingle on the inside of a bend. The water was low now, and seen from the distance of the farmhouse it had that skeleton-service look I remembered from the summer months on the Yorkshire stone rivers of my youth. But storm water tumbling down from the fell can quickly bring a spate, and the Esk then is a river to be treated with respect.

We told each other after tea, tired from the long drive in my Morris Oxford, that we probably wouldn't fish tonight but go to bed early to be ready for tomorrow – although we both knew that tiredness was never going to get in the way of a first look at the river. But we did decide at least to postpone the trials on Uncle Reggie's inventions. And so, after a thumping dinner served by Mrs Marsden, we said we'd just give it a short go and made our way down in the dusk.

We took adjacent 'dubs', exhilarated and unwatched, hearing each other's reel now and then scratch the silence between the bleating up on the fell of some unsettled sheep. It was a dark night, with scarcely any moon on the water, and a slight damp chill on the light breeze that kept you feeling in that state of almost paradoxical alert that comes as a stage of extreme tiredness.

The sea trout were much in evidence. Probably seventy per cent of them were 'whitling', fish returning to the river after less than a year at sea and weighing between half a pound and a pound. Nearly all the rest would have spent a full year at sea and have weighed between a pound and a half and five pounds; but there were just a few which had been at sea for two years or more, and these would be like the big fellow that Mrs Marsden's gentleman had brought back for the pot.

That evening I fished a Claret Jay, a Silver Doctor and a Butcher, all on size 10, and there was a constant bustle of excitement. The fish that may have been tucked in beneath overhanging trees and undercut banks in daytime tend to spread out at night. You catch them in the heads and tails of the pools rather than in the faster water, or in deep streamy water under high banks. The technique is to cast across the current and let the flies swing round with it, gradually lengthening the line until you're covering the whole width of the river – which in the case of the Esk presents no problem – and with each cast moving a pace or so downstream.

I had five whitling, all of them worth fish twice their size in the way they charged about the pool, sometimes boring down, sometimes breaking the surface in spectacular leaps. I set them back in the river, but kept three nice fish of about two pounds each. With such good sport on my old split-cane rod and Hardy Perfect reel, I couldn't help wondering if Uncle Reggie's innovations were going to be surplus to requirements. It was an unworthy thought because we were here as guinea pigs at his expense; and to judge from the excitement of this first evening, even guinea pigs with absurd equipment were likely to catch fish.

It was almost lunchtime by the time we came downstairs. Mrs Marsden had been looking forward to a comprehensive chat, but fortunately for us her brother-in-law, who looked after the farm now, had called in and drawn off some of her conversational steam.

She congratulated us both on our catch (Lawrence had brought in three sea trout too) and we pressed her to take what she wanted for herself and Sprat. She reported this to the dog in a special voice, praising our generosity, which it acknowledged, within its limited powers of rejoinder, from its usual position under the kitchen table. Then Mrs Marsden removed the lid of a simmering saucepan and said that she hoped we could manage some portions of her Muncaster Special. This was a rich and colossal stew, containing for all I knew some ten per cent of the local electorate, but so deliciously supplemented with sauce and vegetables that we got through our allocation with flying colours. So much so that Mrs Marsden looked at us with a professional eye and pronounced us good for a couple each of her Eskdale flaps. These were oversized face flannels folded over a mound of sweet stewed apple, and completely demolished our digestive defences.

Perhaps it was the Eskdale flaps, but a mood of procrastination overtook us in respect of Uncle Reggie's inventions. Lawrence and I were both conscious of it, though neither of us would admit it to the other for fear of seeming ungracious to our absent sponsor. So there was a sort of slow bicycle race between us before Lawrence proposed that we go down first to try to mark fish in the river for tonight's excursion; then after tea apply ourselves to the test programme of the Pitremington accessories. I eagerly agreed, and with a more enticing afternoon immediately ahead of us, in a demonstration of *bona fides* we laid out Uncle Reggie's brainchildren in the old laundry adjoining the kitchen which we were using as a fishing room.

We didn't take our rods, but made our way together down the near bank trying to get a sight of sizeable fish. There was almost no weed, and with the river not at all high and the sun shining, the water was bright and clear. We spotted quite a few big sea trout, some riding the current, some skulking under tree roots or boulders close to the bank. Often, as they saw us, they would turn and flick away, then settle head into the stream a little further off. We marked their position in relation to a tree or post on the other bank, in order to get the angle of cast when we came down again at night.

In the third pool down we saw a really big one – it looked all of ten pounds – close to the bottom beside a rocky shelf.

'Target for tonight,' Lawrence said.

We backed away. I suspect we were both wondering how we should decide which one of us should cast for him. It occurred to me, slyly, that it might be hard to deny it to the one who assumed the burden of Uncle Reggie's Armsplint Rod. But then perhaps the prize was too alluring to be entrusted to ludicrous equipment.

We saw other good fish in our patrol of the bank, four of about five pounds in the same pool, which would be a suitable distraction for Lawrence if I were allowed first go at the big one. But what was encouragingly apparent was that there were any number of sea trout in the river and more on the way up; and with conditions much the same as the previous evening, the prospects looked enticing.

Walking back to Mrs Marsden's, though gravely tempted by the fish we'd marked, we agreed that we must abide by the call of duty and test out the inventions. It was pleasing to find that Sprat had already partially eaten two of them: the Rotatocard Pop-up Fly Dispenser, fortunately for the dog not yet loaded with hooks, was crumpled cardboard, as was the Loop 'n Save Double-Sided Cast Compartment Pack. I reproached the animal, hypocritically, but it backed away with such a contrite and appealing look that I hadn't the heart to report its misdemeanours to Mrs Marsden. And as Lawrence fair-mindedly pointed out, it might be imped-ing the march of science but it hadn't exactly bitten a wing off the Spitfire.

The truth was there was no sign of inspiration amid Uncle Reggie's litany of discovery. Resignedly we apportioned responsibility for the different items, with no feeling of participation in great events. On the contrary, it was dis-tressingly apparent that Uncle Reggie's flair for the imprac-tical and unnecessary was in a class of its own. But theory and application are two different things and we felt con-strained to honour our obligations and give the inventions a fair crack of the rod.

Disingenuously, and with my mind still on the whopper, I volunteered to try out the Armsplint. It was a curious idea, with its basis in economy and flexibility. It's true that in the dark someone of no experience is fractionally more likely to run into something with a conventional fly rod than he is with his outstretched arm, and of course there's a saving on the rodcase which is already provided by your sleeve. Uncle Reggie's device involved a long splint with rings, worn un-der the arm, through which you threaded the line in the normal way. The reel, with two additional thongs to hold it firm, was positioned close to your armpit. There was an immediate minor inconvenience to be considered, which had somehow escaped them at the drawing board, and that was that the reel handle was pointing outwards; so that to manipulate the reel in the conventional way you had to adopt a similar position to that of a baboon scratching itself. Or get used to reloading the reel.

Attached into a ferrule underneath the wrist was a split cane rod tip about two foot long, which you gripped and controlled like a minuscule brook rod, though the length of your arm gave you considerable leverage when casting, provided you freed line from your reel with your left hand. It wasn't by any conceivable stretch of the imagination a good idea, and probably involved a serious thrombosis risk, but it was vaguely workable. More to the point, I was reasonably sure that I could get out enough line to wheel a Blue Boy or a Silver Doctor across the snout of Mr Big.

'I'll have a go at the rod,' I said to Lawrence, 'and the Kneepad Lunch Box.' This was an oblong container with a foam rubber top which you wore like an ascended shinpad, with one strap that went round the top of your calf and another long one like a suspender that attached to your belt, either pulling down your trousers or keeping your sandwiches steady just below your knee. It wasn't an item that I looked at with much confidence, but there have been moments in all our fishing careers when we'd have been glad of kneepads, and there are always moments when we'd be glad of lunch.

'Can I tempt you with the Forage Cap Pencil Torch?' Lawrence asked.

'You can indeed,' I said.

This was a device of fractional appeal, though not perhaps in the way that Uncle Reggie intended it. The forage cap, though it looks both ridiculous and insecure, will stay positioned on your head without discomfort and that cleft in the top might actually be intended for the storage of a pencil torch, which snuggles down unobtrusively, at the same time releasing a discreet beam over the forehead. It's a gentleman's version of the Davy Lamp, and can be brought into more precise play for the tying of flies at night. (In this respect Uncle Reggie's Luminous Blade Scissor Pack didn't quite bring home the bacon.)

The Lay Priest Bolt Gun was a bit too much of a good thing. I believe something similar is in commission in abattoirs, and the idea was that you pressed the mouth of the barrel against the nape of the fish's neck and pulled the trigger. A metal cylinder, propelled by a very strong spring, drove uncompromisingly into the fish's neck and dispatched it without argument. The trouble with Uncle Reggie's model was that it would virtually decapitate any fish weighing less than about twenty-five pounds. We tried it out on Mrs Marsden's kitchen table and it made a crater like a small meteorite. Still, I didn't want to prejudge anything, so I strapped on the shoulder holster and resolved to give it a fair trial should the limitations of my other equipment allow the opportunity.

Looking round the remaining inventions it was apparent that of the two of us Lawrence's was the role of the Heavy Brigade. The Puffemoff Midge Repellent Apparatus was a hefty affair, although this was not entirely inappropriate since the midge can be the angler's heftiest problem. But Uncle Reggie's device was confrontational in the extreme.

The focal point was the cardboard-burning incinerator, protected by a thin coat of asbestos, which you strapped to your back. Its purpose was to generate smoke, on much the same principle that beekeepers use to keep bees quiet. The upward current of the smoke depended on two sets of bellows strapped behind your legs which were operated by bending your knees. The smoke generated by the smouldering cardboard was thus forced up a thin pipe, approximately corresponding to an external spine, which was attached to a headpiece something, in terms of design, between a crown of thorns and the Statue of Liberty's hat – but with the spikes open-ended. Out of these egress points smoke erupted as from a mini industrial landscape, to give the wearer and the midges an almost equally bad time. To add to the package, there were some Smokestart Safety Spills in a waterproof wrapper that the dog had for some reason overlooked.

Lawrence thought he'd better put the Cementigrip Suction Waders on first. These were fairly conventional-looking affairs, with soles composed of rubber pads like halves of extremely large squash balls. As a gripping agent they worked excellently, but when Lawrence pulled on the waders and lowered his weight on to the tenacious soles he was completely unable to move. I had to help him out of the waders, which remained like sentinels on Mrs Marsden's floor until they were chiselled off by her brother-in-law the following day.

There remained the swordfish-resistant Walnut Floataway Jacket, which was a variant of the lifejacket principle. We had no means in Eskdale of testing the veracity of the swordfish claim, but the equipment looked robust enough, made of some sort of reinforced fibre (the 'walnut' was descriptive both of shape and appearance). If the Cementigrip boots let you down and you tipped up in the flood water, you'd probably float for long enough to paddle yourself to safety. But it would be a race against time, because the walnut let in water around both the shoulders and the hips.

Mrs Marsden wished us luck as we set off after dinner for the river, equipped with our bizarre accessories. Obviously slightly baffled by the provenance of such stuff, she made approving remarks about it and even congratulated us on our ingenuity, which when you're strapped to possibly the most idiotic devices ever to appear on a river bank isn't what you want to hear. Then, just at the last moment, she twigged that my kneepads were designed to double up as lunch boxes, and although we'd only just surmounted dinner we had to wait while she made eight tongue sandwiches and crammed them into place.

When we reached the shingle bank opposite where we'd seen the very big fish, I helped Lawrence light up the midge-repeller. We got the cardboard smouldering and soon, after some vigorous contortions with the bellows, quite strong columns of smoke began to billow up around his head. Their effect on the enemy was impossible to gauge, since it

34

was a virtually midge-free night, but they made Lawrence cough uncontrollably. I therefore took it upon myself, since negotiation was for the moment out of the question, to award first go at the whopper to the angler impeded by the Armsplint Night Rod.

I fitted myself up and, cheered at the last moment by Lawrence's spluttering approval, bowled my cast into the river. A sea trout of about a pound took the Butcher first time. I managed to get him in after a rather uncomfortable few minutes and dispatched him with a single shot with the Lay Priest Bolt Gun.

When I was organised again, Lawrence, who had been watching behind me, moved off towards the next pool, smoking like a tramp steamer but coughing much less now than before.

It happened that the big fish had moved out into the river, towards my bank, keeping much the same distance from the head of the pool as we'd seen him that afternoon. It also happened that he had a well-developed sense of the absurd, because he took my Blue Boy, served up rather flimsily by the Armsplint, with a crashing take, leapt into the air like a pole-vaulter, smashed back into the water and took out my line in a high-velocity whine that burned the palm of my hand as I tried to check it.

I battled with no real hope, with lengths of line beginning to be festooned around me. Perhaps because I had no expectations, I took rash chances over his breaking me; but for some extraordinary reason he didn't, and after a little over quarter of an hour I realised I was in with a chance. I shouted for Lawrence at the top of my voice. Uncle Reggie or no Uncle Reggie, with a ten-pound sea trout on the line, some conventions were going to have to be observed. And one of them was my cane-rimmed landing net, which Lawrence had picked up to fan the smoke away from around his head and carried off down river.

My encounter had degenerated into something close to a tug of war, redeemed only by the fact that I appeared to be winning it, when I heard footfalls on the shingle, approaching at a run. Lawrence was on the way. As he came through the trees that lined the bank between us, I saw also he was on fire. The Walnut Floataway Jacket was exuding smoke from every pore, wafting up amid the authorised output from the Crown of Thorns.

'Look out,' I shouted, 'you're burning.'

Lawrence didn't reply. He threw down my landing net, lurched to his left and disappeared into the river with a loud hissing noise.

The number of items beneath the surface of the Esk that it was essential for me to bring ashore had now increased to two. I thought for a moment that the sea trout had got clear when, in the distraction of seeing Lawrence partially alight, I had relaxed my hold on him. But as I took up the slack of the line he was still there. The renewed pressure sent him firing off downstream again.

My dilemma of course was whether I should immediately abandon my battle with the sea trout and go, rather inexpertly, in search of Lawrence or trust to the efficacy of the Walnut Floataway Jacket to help him to the bank. My lifesaving skills are fairly limited and, if we were facing a disaster, my taking to the water might only increase the casualty list to two. I dithered and I hoped; but hoped with such an urgent upward thrust that it must have been picked up in Headquarters as a prayer. I saw Lawrence break the surface, not too far from the bank, and begin to scramble back to safety. Less than a minute later he was behind me with the landing net, dripping, his accoutrements still more or less in place, his face smudged black. In the beam of my Forage Cap Pencil Torch he looked like some ill-conceived Commando.

I caught the fish and laid him brutally to rest with a

shot from Uncle Reggie's Bolt Gun, elated then suddenly ashamed at the coarseness of his dispatch. I lowered him into the water's edge to wash the blood from the remains of his head and as I stepped back towards the bank, my foot slipped on a wet boulder and I fell heavily, throwing the fish ahead of me as I went and pushing out my other arm to break my fall. More marks to Uncle Reggie. The Armsplint broke, but not the arm, an inversion of the normal rule; my knees, bolstered both by Uncle Reggie's kneepads and Mrs Marsden's tongue sandwiches, smote against the rocks as against thistledown. The trials were fairly made.

We walked back to the house with our catch and the battered nucleus of the inventions. We could, in honesty, claim some success, but we had reservations about recommending mass production. We decided what to say to Uncle Reggie. For the rest of the week we could revert to the fishing we understood.

At the de-briefing in the dining room of Pitremington Hall, we went through the items one by one – even those which had seen service only in Sprat's mouth. Our overall report could only be discouraging. We couldn't even blame the conditions for the disappointing showing, since Lawrence and I had fared extremely well with our old and unenlightened gear. Our summing up, though of course we didn't put it quite so bluntly, was that the range was almost certainly the silliest that had so far been devised.

Uncle Reggie took it well, but he could always see encouragement in the blackest news. Even the report of Sprat's eating two of his inventions.

'Very useful,' he said, 'I'm more than grateful to you. That dog's the key. You can't get away from animals or sex. People are gluttons for both of them.'

He abandoned the fishing ideas and marketed a product called Down Sir, which had a big success in the stockbroker belt for the protection of bitches in season – and might have had an even bigger one, some people thought, for the protection of the stockbrokers' wives. Uncle Reggie sold out for a notable profit. By then, as usual, he badly needed the money. Necessity, we reminded him, is the mother of invention.

'No,' said Uncle Reggie, 'necessity is the invention of the mother.'

3
Giant Waders

My whole schoolmastering career, both before and after my marriage to Helen Wilkes, was spent at Combermere, a boys' preparatory school in Dorset. There I stayed quite happily, perhaps not altering the face of traditional education, but at least helping to foster its complexion. The leopard may not change its spots, but it shouldn't be allowed to pick them.

The school belonged to the Choldertons, first the one who initially employed me, then his nephew, and on the principle that if you own the drawing-pins you might as well put up the notices, each assumed the role of headmaster, the elder, at the end of the war, ceding to the younger. Mr Cholderton senior was a dedicated fly fisherman, and our common interest cemented my position on the staff; so that when his nephew, Henry, took over, he was conditioned to my enthusiasms. I was allowed days off to accommodate special fishing treats, and I gave some of the older boys instruction on our little section of the Axe. This not only went down well with the parents but brought me invitations to fish in the holidays.

The staff were an odd assortment. The credentials for doing well were not primarily academic – most people could keep a few pages ahead of their class – and some masters' technique was quirky by the standards of today's more sophisticated profession. Yet the effectiveness of the teaching, to judge from the examination results, was very adequate. The syllabus was about force-feeding, the teaching was about digestion; and those who were good at it hit upon some rapprochement of personality and method which was not easy to define. The criterion was only whether it worked; so that it hardly mattered that when a more able-bodied establishment reassembled after the war several members of Common Room were wearing gowns that were more likely relics of the blackout than of university degrees.

The support group, ranged over all the responsibilities of running such a place, had some long-serving stalwarts. One was a simpleton called Jack, officially referred to as a pantryman, who variously looked after the boiler, put on a white coat and served unhygienically in hall, cleared the gutters and played conkers or marbles with the boys. His access to the boiler meant that he could bake his conkers and he tended to make short work of the shinier but softer opposition which the boys dislodged with footballs and croquet mallets from the chestnuts in the drive. His star contender, which dominated the 1949 season, was reassembled after its eventual defeat and mounted in a glass case in the cricket pavilion. I always felt a similar fate might be awaiting Jack, because it became a great joke among his opponents to swing over their conkers and hit him on the top of the head. He didn't seem to mind, perhaps because he often won without having to put his own conkers much at risk.

The domestic lynchpin, at least in my early years, was the cook-housekeeper, Miss Craigie, a Mount Etna in contour and suppressed passion, though with fewer vineyards on the lower slopes. I mentioned in my earlier memoir that she acquired the nickname of 'The Holiday Let' because, as related to me by Mr Congleton, the French master, the *on dit* went that if you took her on holiday, she'd let you. Quite who the *on* was who *dit* something so shabby was for a while a matter of conjecture. It finally turned out to be the bursar.

He had taken her, Mr Congleton told me, for a few days to a hotel in Swanage. It had been rather like taking part in a pancake race, Mr Congleton salaciously reported – as the pancake. I asked to hear no more about the bursar's conquest; but watching him in the company of Miss Craigie, I feared that what Mr Congleton had told me might be true. Although he looked more like George I than Errol Flynn, the sidling confidence about his attitude towards her seemed to confirm there had been an exchange of secrets. Worse, there was a lecherous suction in the way he looked at her, which you felt might suddenly hoover off her overall. So it was no surprise that when it came to casting for the school pantomime, a dreadful entertainment that was the brainchild of the bursar, Miss Craigie was up there in the numbers. The rest of us awaited the call resignedly, but the headmaster asked us to remember that it was the bursar who had recently presented Combermere with the science schools. The least we could do was to support his pantomime.

Science schools? This was a bit much. A wooden cabin, yes, had been erected in the stable yard and equipped, admittedly at the bursar's expense, with some rudimentary science props – bunsen burners, a few chemicals, the wherewithal for some physics experiments, and what we called, in the context of the bursar's conversation, the blunt retorts. When I remonstrated with the headmaster, he merely said that President Garfield's upbringing had been partly spent in a building of equally modest construction and it had proved no obstacle to a term in the White House.

This being so, arrangements had been made for a Mr Skey to join the staff. Apart from being an adventurous hand with the litmus paper, Mr Skey held the record for the largest roach caught in Somerset. As none of the rest of us had much idea about science, he seemed as sound a choice as any to supervise the bursar's cradle of invention.

The bursar's theatrical experience had been limited to a brief appearance, during his City days, with the Eastcheap Gilbert and Sullivan Players. He had figured unprominently in a production of *The Pirates of Penzance*, but from his eagerness about the pantomime, which he had been writing himself, he had obviously succumbed to the grip of the greasepaint. In the fervour of creative thought, he started to affect a rolltop sweater and a suede jacket instead of his usual hardy annuals, a matching tweed jacket and waistcoat and a pair of very dark grey flannels with icebreaker creases. We gathered that Jack and the Beanstalk was the chosen topic. We waited uneasily for further particulars.

Casting took place quite early in the Michaelmas term. The bursar invited us, individually, for 'a few words' in his office. Miss Craigie was first in; I was eleventh. The bursar and I enjoyed a rather combative relationship, and I had been beginning to hope I had been excluded from the production in the mistaken belief that I should mind.

Not so.

'I'd like to make something of your fly-fishing skills,' the bursar said.

'A little out of season,' I said, pleasantly enough.

'I was hoping,' the bursar went on, 'you might cast over the audience with a huge rod, and then cast into the wings and we'll fit on an inflatable trout. I thought we might call you Giant Waders.'

I had suffered in pantomime before – when my father had mounted the stage at the Bournemouth Pavilion and danced with Maid Marion. The scars of childhood last the longest. Now the bursar was proposing to open them again.

'There's a technical difficulty,' I said. 'You have to have as much space behind you as you intend to cast in front. I don't want to hurl the scenery into the audience.'

The bursar looked impatient. 'Well, you know about fishing. What's that low swoopy cast they do in Scotland?'

'It's called a Spey cast. But it depends on lifting your line off the water.'

'Well, we'll work something out. They'll expect you to do something pretty nifty.' He consulted his watch. 'Can you manage stilts?'

'I've never tried,' I said, 'but I expect I'd break my legs all right.'

'They wouldn't be very tall stilts,' the bursar said. 'Otherwise you'd be up in the rafters. You're a bit of a streak as it is.'

I didn't like this reference to my personal appearance, especially from someone whose own looks caused no spontaneous outbreak of violins. But I lay back, as it were, and thought of science.

'Giant Waders?' the bursar asked eventually, watching me in an predatory way.

'Fine,' I said.

Typically, it was one of the boys in my form who told me at breakfast a few days later that the pantomime had been retitled *Aladdin and the Beanstalk* and that the Easterner would be played by Mr Congleton.

I thought we should have heard this ourselves from the producer. I saw him just as I was going into school and told him I'd caught up with the press release. The slyness of my shaft eluded him.

'What press release?' he said.

I walked silently into my formroom and, making sure he was following me, closed the door in his face.

Mr Congleton was quite thick with the bursar, and it had always been on the cards that he'd land one of the plums – even at the price of transforming it into a damson. But I had to admit there was a touch of flair about making him Aladdin. His morbidly sallow complexion would look rather appropriate under the lampshade hat. Certainly it was noticeably better casting than Miss Craigie as Bo Peep.

'Bo Peep,' I'd said pleadingly to the headmaster when the news got out. 'What's he thinking about? Aren't there usually connotations of a lack of size? Of littleness?'

He shrugged. 'It's a question of how you're using the word "little". Do you mean "little" as in "diminutive", or "little" as in "a little on the big side"?'

I could see he'd been got at by subsidised science.

The musical accompaniment was to be provided by Mr Westacott, who came in from Chard to service the mowers and had a good local reputation as a workmanlike pianist. His instrument, which he said he preferred to use rather than the headmaster's Bechstein, was an Upright Oldham, a little-known make that looked like a boarding-house washstand. His selection, however, in preference to the Music Staff was likely to raise a few eyebrows, especially when it was rumoured that Miss Craigie had put in a good word for him. (We called them the Music Staff, but in fact they were an assortment of part-timers who came in to teach the obvious instruments, just to keep the parents happy.) I think the headmaster must have spoken to the bursar, because we were then told that both Mr Pringle on trumpet and Miss Advani on 'cello would be joining Mr Westacott in the orchestra pit.

Meanwhile we began to learn our lines. Captain Corkhill, the maths master, and I would pace up and down the drive trying to keep our scripts behind our backs and testing one another. The Captain had been cast as Baron Badlad, and he was to be attended in his malpractices by the two Axemen, one played by Mr Skey, the other by the PT instructor. This allusion to our local river gives you a flavour of the bursar's wit, which was measured in planks.

The run was scheduled for three performances just before the boys went home for Christmas. The plan was that a proportion of each night's audience would be drummed up from the surrounding district and invited to part with money for some deserving charity, though were there any justice in the world the charity would have been themselves. On Miss Craigie's recommendation, the Audience Recruiting Officer was to be our old friend Major Macdonald-Macdonald, the one-armed President of the Winsham and Chard Highland Dancing Society, where – in the company of Miss Craigie – I had once spent a best-forgotten evening. There were predictable jokes among the staff about the Major being a safe half-pair of hands, which were a little tasteless considering the good fellow had lost his limb in the service of his country. His wife, Myrna, offered her services as prompter and, after a week or two of rehearsals, began to attend our evening workouts to keep us textually on the rails.

The PT instructor, in addition to his responsibilities as one of Captain Corkhill's Axemen, gave me lessons in walking on stilts. Merely in the interests of ordinary dignity these lessons took place in private. I made it a condition that not even the bursar would be allowed to witness my discomfiture, though I told myself that it could be no worse than one's first effort with chest waders in a full-running salmon river. You might lose your footing more painfully, but at least you wouldn't drown. In the event I managed much better than expected and on my final test did three clockwise laps round the science hut in less than two minutes fifty. The PT instructor pronounced me stageworthy, slightly, I suspect, to the disappointment of the bursar. He still had the last laugh, however. He had put me in charge of the audience participation song.

This pantomime evergreen is as effective a vehicle for mutual embarrassment in the theatre as any yet devised – and the theatrical profession is not unresourceful. My own number, preceded by my casting demonstration, was entitled 'Watch Out, Mr Trout'. Its sentiments were compact, its verse construction unsophisticated. My role was a fusion of vocalist and cheer leader, both on stilts. The potential for self-degradation, in front of pupils, colleagues and the Eightsome stylists of the Winsham and Chard Highland Dancing Society, was genuinely limitless.

But camaraderie is a wonderful thing. Ill-assorted and incompetent as we were, with an inept script and lamentably sung songs, we found ourselves enjoying it all. We started to become tremendously 'Green Room', I even heard Captain Corkhill address Miss Craigie once as 'ducky'. Even the bursar's presiding vanity seemed, in the excitement of performance, a sort of leadership.

The boys of course adored it. The prospect of sir making himself a laughing stock is always appealing to the young, at least on school ground. In the holidays, as I found on more than one occasion, boy and master identify together as school, and each can feel let down, in terms of outside opinion, by the other's poor performance. When I went fishing with their parents in the holidays, the same boys who longed for Giant Waders to fall into the Upright Oldham would have died a thousand deaths – unless they were in some way successfully competing with me – had I not impressed the company with rod and line. At home, or in the fishing lodge, my embarrassment was theirs. On the boards in the school pantomime my embarrassment was strictly mine.

Mr Judd, the carpenter, supported by a posse of local

artists, did wonders with the sets. There was just the right cosiness about the exterior of Bo Peep's cottage in the Village Square, even if the dimensions looked a little suspect when she was holding court outside. The façade of Badlad Castle, outside Winsham, was Weightwatcher-Vanbrugh *à point* – gloriously baroque but not quite excessive – and the Glade in the Forest on the Way to Transylvania was a cathedral of oaks through whose dense overhang of branches the sun shone in mysterious brilliance. Here it was that I was to involve the house both in my casting demonstration and in the performance of 'Watch Out, Mr Trout'. We were to be assisted by a huge plywood prompt board which Mr Judd would winch down from above the front of the stage.

A handful of the very senior boys were allowed to assist backstage, and a lucky four from Form III – Leavis, Jacobs, Attlee and Wedderburn – joined the cast as Bo Peep's sheep. Miss Advani provided some restrained arrangements for the songs, the Crewkerne Amateur Dramatic Society made available its entire portfolio of costumes, and Miss Craigie's wig was styled by Maison Jeanne of Winsham. The Macdonald-Macdonalds were reported to be fairly herding them in. We looked all set for a smash – of one sort or the other.

At the first night, after a promising dress rehearsal, the bursar was tense but poised to be triumphant. The curtain went up on the Village Square in Winsham with Bo Peep a little down in the mouth. Her sheep, she reported, were missing. Widow Twanky, played by Mr Manisty (Geography), reassured her. The drama was away on its switchback course of novelty and invention. We saw a brusque exchange with the Baron at the gates of Castle Badlad, a tearful appeal by Bo Peep to the villagers, and Scene 1 reached its close.

When the curtain rose again, it was to reveal Jack dressed

as a wizard, a sort of Yellow Pages in a pointed hat, who disclosed that there was a specialist in sheep recovery, Mr Aladdin, living with a perspicacious talking vegetable in a cave in Transylvania. This news (not to mention the delivery) only upset Bo Peep. She said she could never afford the fare. But after a series of noisy junketings the villagers raised the money. Bo Peep wept in gratitude, kissed most of the company, and prepared to leave for Transylvania.

It was in the Glade in the Forest on the Way to Transylvania that things started to go wrong. I was by now in an agony of apprehension, balanced on my half-stilts, fingering my rod and beset by the imminence of the audience participation number. The bursar, irritatingly cocky, was standing in the wings in front of me accompanying the modulations of his script with wavy gestures. I saw Miss Craigie look round the huge oak glade, sigh and declare that it reminded her of her beloved Scotland. This, it had always struck me, was a constructional flaw. She had hitherto led us to suppose she was a dyed-in-the-wool Dorset sheeptender, and now here she was somewhere between Winsham and Transylvania, wearing a kilt and rooting for the Old Enemy. Besides, as something of a regular myself on the night sleeper north, I didn't, on looking round the glade, get the same topographical tug. It was a device of course, and probably the least cumbersome way to get round the fact that the only song Miss Craigie was prepared to sing in public was 'Loch Lomond'.

The chances of Miss Craigie fluffing the lyrics of 'Loch Lomond' were nil, so it was a reasonable moment for the prompter to take time off to hold the ladder while the carpenter hoisted into place the billboard containing the lyrics of 'Watch Out, Mr Trout', which was the next feature scheduled for the Glade. So as Miss Craigie, in a Force 8 contralto, debated the alternative routes to the Highlands,

Mrs Macdonald-Macdonald left the prompter's chair, to which her dog Fortinbras was securely tied, and went to Mr Judd's assistance.

Fortinbras was a smooth-coated dog with a very pointed face that was ideal for examining other animals' parts. It was a nice dog, but a dog whose curiosity could sometimes get the better of its obedience. As it watched Miss Craigie singing her kilt off in the Glade, it became aware that in the temporary absence of its mistress a closer look, a guest appearance even, was an available option. So it ventured out on to the boards, towing the chair behind it.

This was a great success with the more frivolous elements of the audience, less so with the animal's co-proprietor, Major Macdonald-Macdonald, who was seated in the front row alongside the headmaster. A breakdown in pet discipline was not the Major's cup of tea.

He stood up.

'Myrna,' he shouted, 'Fortinbras is on the stage.'

Mr Westacott, put off by this interruption no more than a yard or two away, faltered at the Upright Oldham. Mr Pringle's trumpet died to a brass yawn. Miss Advani, revolving to keep her options open, kept up a sort of caretaker *pizzicato* on the 'cello.

'Fortinbras,' the Major bellowed, giving each syllable equal and extended emphasis, 'get off, you pointed sod.'

This was unexpected competition for Miss Craigie's rendering of 'Loch Lomond'. It also produced an unfortunate chain reaction. Myrna Macdonald-Macdonald abandoned her supervision of the ladder, which fell sideways against the back of the flat depicting some of the nobler oaks, which in turn fell forwards on to the stage, revealing a number of the production staff in informal pose. The carpenter lost control of the lyric board of 'Watch Out, Mr Trout', which crashed down within inches of Miss Craigie, then toppled forward into the orchestra pit, dispersing the trio and causing some superficial damage to the Upright Oldham. It was followed almost immediately, like a windfall apple, by the carpenter. Fortinbras, startled, struck off backstage, still towing his chair.

Miss Craigie, like the good trouper she was, stood by the dictum that the show must go on. She hitched up her kilt and broke into her number again. Mr Pringle and Miss Advani soon caught up with her, although Mr Westacott was deflected by urgent repairs to the Upright Oldham.

I looked to see the effect of all this on the bursar. He was stooping forward, pressing the top of his head, as if to force it down his neckshaft into the concealment of his chest. The word 'rout' was written all over the production. I think I went mad. Miss Craigie deserved some moral support. I decided to take a hand.

Striding on in my half-stilts, clutching my rod, I entered what was left of the glade. There was a surge of applause. Miss Craigie, singing of the bonny banks, smilingly nodded acknowledgement of my show of solidarity. Bringing my line back through the gap in the scenery, I sizzled it out over the audience. Major Macdonald-Macdonald was still upright in the front row, shouting to his wife to re-establish control of Fortinbras, and I think in recovering my line I may just have clipped the back of his head. It may have been this that got the better of his self-control, or it may have been his wife's ham-fistedness in detaching Fortinbras from the chair and then accidentally letting go of him so that he reappeared on stage and started barking at Miss Craigie. Most likely it was a combination of the two, though from what I knew of the Major's makeup, the double public disgrace of indiscipline from his dog and incompetence from his wife would have weighed the heavier. He charged the stage.

This was a bemedalled veteran of the Western Front, a man you wouldn't stop without several rolls of barbed wire and a company of sharpshooters. In fact he was after Fortinbras, but Mr Westacott thought he was after me and tried to block him with the Upright Oldham. The Major brushed it aside like a matchbox, and scrambled up the parapet that separated the orchestra from the stage. Something told me, with clear enunciation, that the time had come to make for the wings. I threw down my rod and went as fast as my stilts would carry me. I heard the bursar calling 'Curtain, curtain,' but the carpenter, whose responsibility this was, still lay immobilised on stage.

All seemed lost. But then occurred a series of miracles. The brief intervention by Mr Westacott had added crucial seconds on to the Major's charge, with the result that when he got on to the stage not only had I left it but his wife had appeared helter-skelter, snatched up Fortinbras, and rushed off again with the dog under her arm. Even the carpenter was beginning to crawl slowly towards the wings. So the Major, with audience interest behind him at fever pitch, found himself face to face with Miss Craigie with no mission left to perform. To our amazement he began to join Miss Craigie in a duet, singing in a very decent and unselfconscious baritone. Miss Craigie, beaming, opened up like a giant Venus flytrap and captivated the audience's affections in one swallow. Together the soloists came front stage, their arms extended forward in a trident, as if to spear the participation of the house. They succeeded. At first rather wavering and apologetic, the singing gathered authority, then swelled out of all proportion, backed by a rhythmic clapping of hands. From the safety of the wings I couldn't believe it; and this was but the start of Providence's intervention.

The bursar turned angrily to confront me.

'Who told you to go on stage?' he snapped. 'Your number's cancelled.' He addressed the waiting staff. 'Giant Waders is grounded. After this, straight into Aladdin's cave.'

Mr Congleton, being helped on with his eighteen-inch fingernails and looking terribly unpromising in his lampshade hat, gazed at us uncomprehendingly.

The bursar allowed himself another venomous glance in my direction. 'And that applies to the rest of the run,' he said.

Basking in my reprieve, I followed the next part of the drama from the bursar's personal chair. Miss Craigie and the Major were accorded a stupendous standing ovation. The Major kissed Miss Craigie gallantly on the cheek and returned as hero to the place in the audience he had left as hothead. The curtain fell, the change of scenery rumbled into place, Mr Congleton, in a long silk gown with storks and rustic bridges all over it, rested his fingernails on a lacquer table left centre in the cave, subdued lighting came on and the curtain rose.

It was revealed to us in this scene that the bursar had pushed back the boundaries of wit and that what we were intended to suppose would be a beanstalk was in fact bean's talk. A speaking vegetable, played from behind a screen by the headmaster's mother, divulged the whereabouts of Bo Peep's sheep. The linen cupboard at Castle Badlad. The news had an emotional effect on Bo Peep which Mr Congleton's singing did little to relieve.

So it was back for the confrontation with the Baron, who was luckily out shopping when Bo Peep and a squad of Winsham villagers advanced on his castle. The Axemen's loyalty faltered. They'd let out the sheep, they said, they hadn't been happy at the way the Baron had removed them. So the Baron returned to find the sheep sprung, his hitmen turned against him, and quite a chunk of the population of Winsham asking him what he proposed to do about it. His answer was to shout at them, much as his *alter ego*, Captain Corkhill, taught mathematics.

It got him nowhere. With a triumphal chorus Bo Peep and the villagers returned to the Village Green. There the cast, paired off for the finale in ascending order of importance, took up position on the town hall steps. As Miss Craigie, arm in arm with Mr Congleton, reached her place, three performers to the left of where I was standing arm in arm with Jack, I thought the house must collapse. The cheering told me there wasn't a red-blooded man in the hall who wouldn't have given his left arm to be taking Miss Craigie off to Swanage. Except of course Major Macdonald-Macdonald, who was impaired by considerations of availability.

And, need I add, myself.

4

A Matter of Honour

I come to the conclusion, after a tidy few laps around the circuits of experience, that most people cheat. Not all the time of course – but at some time or another, at something. This is not to say that sportsmanship is a myth, but possibly the sportsman needs re-defining – as someone, maybe, who gets moral uplift from cheating unsuccessfully. We anglers are in the main paragons of fair play (if you can disregard that awkward truth about blood sports that the quarry, not of its own choosing, has rather more at stake); but we are exposed to two of the more fatal enemies of honour – competitiveness and seclusion. My escapade with Moby is a case in point.

Moby was a very large brown trout which must have outweighed any of its immediate fraternity by some three pounds. It lived in the River Wylye, in a deep hole below a footbridge near the village of Hanging Langford. Its capture was the secret dream of those who fished that stretch of the water – a principled crew, who unanimously condemned the postman for trying to depth-charge their leviathan with an old bicycle frame. One of their number was Captain Hector Striding, a hero on the playing fields of yesteryear and the grandfather of one of the less appealing boys at

Combermere, an orphan called Michael Striding, known to everyone as 'Sobs'. He wasn't rude, sullen or ostentatious, but he was pathetic and irritating; and that's a bad combination. He was, to use a well-worn phrase, 'his own worst enemy', which was misplaced effort at Combermere where there were always plenty of candidates to take the burden off his shoulders. Because I gave fishing instruction to the wretched creature and perhaps, too, because I was to some extent protective towards him, I found myself invited to the Wylye Valley by the Captain for an end-season outing on the river. It was not an invitation that I accepted with an easy conscience, for Sobs was not a boy to whom one warmed. I have always tried to set my face against victimisation; but it can sometimes tell you something about the victim.

We set off in my car immediately after morning school on Saturday. Our departure, viewed coolly from the front steps by both the headmaster and the bursar, was undignified but tempered by the obvious goodwill I enjoyed among members of my form, five of whom volunteered to push the car. They stuck with it for almost a hundred yards until it began to make convulsive snatches at combustion. Then, with a supernatural backfire, it sprang to life and, leaving two of the pushers face downwards on the drive, carried us out of the school gates and on to the road to Chard. The embarrassed Sobs slowly emerged above the collar of his tweed jacket, extricated a school atlas and a Letts Schoolboy's diary from his night case, and began to quiz me on the populations of the world. 'Miles out, sir,' he'd say, or, 'I'll give you a hint, sir. It's more than Nicaragua but less than China.' Assisted by this bracketing, I would then be twenty million out. As we drove along the A303, I floundered over the lengths of the world's principal rivers, rallied over capitals, and scored several very near misses over London lighting-up times. Annoyingly, Sobs seemed to view my cross-examination as a knowledge contest between himself and me, in which I was beginning to be exposed as grossly ill-informed while he was notionally outpointing me on little more than an ability to read.

We overshot the entrance to the Striding property as I was considering my selection for the fourteenth highest mountain in the world. I had been relying on Sobs for directions once we reached the immediate vicinity of his grandfather's house, so I was just a little irked to find him asking why we'd driven past. We turned round, went back through the village and up past a lodge. The emotion of regaining the bosom of home was too much for Sobs: he dissolved into tears as we entered the drive and was busily blowing his nose as we came into view of a handsome late Georgian house attended on both sides by ancient cedars.

Mrs Striding came down the steps to greet us, looking at me questioningly as she noticed her grandson's red-rimmed eyes.

'Nice to be back, Michael?' I said, though I wasn't really addressing the boy, but explaining his condition to his grandmother. She gave me a hint of a nod and laid an arm round his shoulder in a gesture of managerial affection.

There was a butler of course, a nice-looking man in early middle age who looked at Sobs paternally and hoped that we'd had a good drive.

'We've been testing each other,' Sobs said.

I watched as he struggled his night case out of the back of the car. The butler walked forward from the steps and took it from him. There was no implied command in the way Sobs proffered it, merely acquiescence in something that was naturally going to happen.

'How's Billy?' Sobs asked.

I assumed this was the butler's son. This was the little gentleman speaking. The child would have asked if Billy was around.

'He's very well, thank you,' the butler said.

We went into the hall. 'My husband's longing to meet you,' Mrs Striding said.

I wondered, if that were so, why the Captain was still practising golf shots about a hundred yards behind the house. As we walked down the lawn towards him, he was striking balls into a net with a wooden club. He was talking to himself, gesticulating, sometimes making little hops into the air. He looked completely mad.

It was a false impression. I was to discover, as my visit progressed, that the Captain was greatly taken with sporting activity – I presume because it reawakened his achievements from the past. When moving about a room, for instance, he would suddenly do a sweeping tennis forearm or backhand drive. Seeing me notice that two of his fingers were bound up with sticking plaster, his wife explained that when practising his off-break action along the first-floor landing, he had misjudged the height of the chandelier.

His talk, too, crackled with sporting allusions. I asked him at lunch about the respective merits of Winchester and Salisbury Cathedrals. His replies were not aesthetically lyrical but he thought that at Salisbury it was probably all of an 8 iron from the west door to the chancel steps. You won't find that in Pevsner.

If the Captain was the overhead volleyer of the partnership, Mrs Striding was Queen of the Baseline. She brought a sense of solidarity to the domestic rallies, which from Sobs's point of view was all to the good because the Captain, though kindly, tended to be over-demanding. He would have expected any grandson of his to be holding his own with racket and club at an early age, and in this Sobs would have been – and known himself to be – a serious disappointment. Dominated by the Captain's sporting expectations, he hoped to present me as a practised angler and, if I were up to form, glean some kudos from the association. What the poor boy couldn't have anticipated was that my other competitive shortcomings were to be so rigorously exposed.

'Hector,' Mrs Striding called out as we approached, 'Mr Hartley and Michael are here.'

Hector Ludorum turned, threw down his club and strode towards me with hand outstretched.

'Do you play football?' he asked. 'Because you're going to have to.'

The words hit me. I couldn't get out of the way.

'I haven't played for years,' I said. 'Fishing's more my thing.'

'Well, we'll go on the river tomorrow morning. But I've said you'd keep goal for the village against Cridland's Biscuits. They're a Warminster outfit.'

'What's happened to the regular goalkeeper?' I asked.

'Bust his arm.'

'He'd still be better with one arm than I would with two.'

The Captain looked at me a little reprovingly.

'Come on,' he said, 'Michael billed you as the great Combermere sportsman.'

I knew I shouldn't have come.

'I haven't any football clothes,' I said desperately.

'You can borrow my boots,' the Captain said. 'They scored two goals against Cambridge.'

'Yes,' I said, 'but they probably had your feet in them. I'm useless. Your team will be disqualified from the league.'

'Not from the Coriolanus League, Division Four,' the Captain replied confidently.

'Couldn't you play?' I asked.

He shook his head. 'I'm the non-playing captain.'

'Well,' I said, hoping I detected a chink. 'Couldn't you be the playing non-captain? Just for once?'

'Wouldn't do. I just lend them the pitch. Keeps them amused on a Saturday afternoon.'

I fell silent. The Captain talked to his grandson as we

walked back into the house, asking him quickfire questions about what he'd been doing without apparently paying much attention to the replies.

On a chair in the hall were a football shirt, a pair of rather long blue football shorts and a Hampshire County Cricket Club sweater.

'There you are,' the Captain said, 'they'll help you keep 'em out.'

We sat down to lunch. Sobs was watching our conversation from the other side of the table like a spectator at a tennis match.

'I hope the defence is reliable,' I said when the Captain had evidently exhausted his companion guide to Salisbury and Winchester Cathedrals.

'The left and right back are mustard,' the Captain reassured me with a mouth full of lettuce. 'They work on the farm here. They're twins. The Andrews brothers.'

Well, at least it was the brothers.

I turned to Mrs Striding.

'Would there be any thick socks?' I asked. My thin socks and suspenders would be an inadequate bridge between trousers and boots that had toyed with the Cambridge University defence.

'There's heaps,' she said. 'Just ask out the back.'

I considered her reply. There is no means of distinguishing, in English speech, between the capital and lower case initial letter. Mrs Striding had definitely said 'There's heaps.' She could either be referring, syntactically incorrectly, to an abundant supply of sockballs at the back of the house, or she must be referring to the butler. I decided to give her the benefit of the doubt and, immediately we got up from the table, I went through the green baize door and surprised the butler eating a jelly.

'Ah, Heeps,' I said, 'I've been told you might be able to find me some thick footballing socks.'

'It's Bennett, sir,' he said with a don't-worry-about-that smile. 'Socks? Yes, sir, in the rod room.'

He escorted me along a passage. The rod room bore the signs of domestic attention. Such rooms are usually at best haphazard, since the eagerness to get out on the river and the tired shedding of one's load at the end of the day are neither of them conducive to good order. Here the waders were hanging neatly together, the assortment of fisherman's flotsam deployed like with like across the table top. Three pairs of scissors lay side by side at exactly the same angle; even an old newspaper, probably used to wrap up a fish, had been folded and pressed in case it contained some item of interest that had caught the Captain's eye.

The butler produced a pair of thick grey socks.

'Will you be needing a cap, sir? The sun's quite strong.'

'I'll be needing a blindfold,' I said.

It was one of those placid golden afternoons with which autumn sometimes supplements the summer, a day of strong light and bold shadow. I walked down to the football field with the Stridings, looking and feeling ridiculous in the Captain's tweed cap, his wife's riding gloves, the Hampshire cricket sweater, the long blue shorts, the rod-room socks and the boots with toecaps of anti-Cambridge dynamite.

The football pitch was half the Captain's allocation to the sporting welfare of the village. The other half was a pleasant tree-lined cricket ground, overlooked by a wooden pavilion, a scoreboard and assorted seats. As we approached across the Stridings' fields, we could see the teams assembled at the back of the pavilion. Our team wore pink and green quartered colours like Battenberg cakes; Cridland's wore biscuit, with black collars and black numbers on the back.

My approach must have been observed with interest. It

could only have been encouraging to Cridland's. I don't know what assurances had been given by the Captain on my behalf, but from a couple of hundred yards I must have looked good for at least a ten-goal deficit against whichever goalmouth I was destined to defend.

Everybody was most polite, I suppose in deference to the Captain. The Andrews brothers came up and introduced themselves. They said the big problem about Cridland's was the centre forward. He'd scored twice as many goals as anyone else in the League. They said they'd do their best to keep him bottled up.

'Which is he?' I asked nervously, having seen someone I hoped it wasn't.

It was. I'd seen men like that in my collection of cigarette card footballers – men with Aston Villa or Arsenal shirts, with perfect physique and centre-parted hair, leg poised in a powerful 'L' above the ball.

The Captain introduced me to the referee, who doubled up as the water bailiff on the stretch we were to fish tomorrow. Then the two captains tossed for ends, I took up my position in the selected goalmouth, warned the Andrews brothers that one or other of them must take the goal kicks, and we were under way. I could see Sobs and his mother positioned to my right about half way down the field. I realised with dismay that in this test of truth and courage I was on trial as Combermere's, as Sobs's champion.

I was much relieved to see that we appeared to be getting the better of things. The Andrews brothers were hard into the tackle, and the supply of ball to the waiting Cridland No 9 was mercifully sparse. Finally, in minute thirty-four, he broke through our defences. For a terrible second I saw the re-enactment of my cigarette cards, the resonant thwack, the perfect harmony of timing. Helpless in the goalmouth, I bent half double to reduce my size as a target and raised my arms, pressed tight together, to shield my face. The ball cannoned against them, hurling me against the back of the net, where I lay for a while until the congratulatory manner of the players who were stooping down to help me to my feet suggested that I had inadvertently pulled off a remarkable save. The ball had powered upwards from my protecting elbows, shot over the bar, over the cricket pavilion and was even now being recovered from the long on position in the far corner of the cricket field.

The Captain came over at half time to offer his congratulations, attributing my inspired performance to his boots. He couldn't resist kicking the ball as he left the centre circle, which, rising from close range, struck one of the Cridland's players in the small of the back. This seemed to be accepted as some form of *droit de seigneur* and the Captain was allowed off with no worse than a few surly looks. We changed ends.

Early in the second half we scored, and should have scored several times more but for the selfishness of our centre forward, a bus driver with the Wilts and Dorset bus company who, used to hours of isolation in his cab and a good deal of invective from motorists in the course of his professional life, had lost sight of the principles of team spirit. It was beginning to look as if we had the measure of the biscuiteers when the Cridland's No 9 intercepted a wayward pass and crashed his way through our defenders. In a desperate attempt to check him, one of the Andrews brothers tripped him and he slithered with a grunting oath almost into our goal. The referee ran up, whistle shrilling, and pointed to the penalty spot.

My instinct was to leave the field and return as fast as I could to Combermere. The penalty spot looked extraordinarily near, the Cridland No 9 at his most menacing, and the ball like a globe of cement. I tried to keep calm. I urged myself to make an intelligent appraisal of my best interests.

My conclusions, in those ensuing moments, ran something like this.

To be struck by a direct, non-angled, blow by the ball at this range was not to be considered. On the plus side, I reckoned that the chances of my adversary firing a second projectile straight at me were no more than one in twenty – probably, in fact, the odds against his doing it accidentally. My choice therefore was to leap either to right or left a fraction of a second before he struck the ball. At worst I would be struck at an angle, with the possible bonus that without serious injury I should thereby prevent the ball from entering the net, or I should look to have made an honourable effort. I also had the huge moral advantage that the taker of the penalty would be expected to have the upper hand. The chances of the goalkeeper, particularly if he were someone as inexperienced and cowardly as myself, were not that good. The fact that I was merely trying to escape injury rather than trying to prevent a goal might easily pass unnoticed. I would dive to my left.

As he positioned the ball on the spot and the rest of my team hung morosely around behind him, I spat on Mrs Striding's riding gloves, took some conspicuous deep breaths, and jerked backwards and forwards with what I hoped was a look of pugnacious confidence. I saw my adversary deciding on his point of aim. He took six or seven paces backwards and scratched the back of his calf with the toe of his other boot. Then, with a noisy exhalation, he accelerated into the kick. I saw his leg strain back, the centre-parted head in perfect concentration above the ball. I soared to my left.

Even as I moved I heard a howl of pain. He had kicked the ground some nine inches behind the ball. The pent-up power of the kick, striking with such force into the ground, was enough to dislodge a memorable divot. The ball, disturbed by the impact on the soil immediately behind it, rolled slowly towards that part of the goal my choice of tactic had now left unattended. Helpless, I saw its energies expire a mere fraction past the line. The referee pranced in to study its position. Dramatically, he blew his whistle and pointed to the centre spot. Cridland's had equalised, and the champion of Combermere had let in the dolliest goal ever scored in the Coriolanus League Division Four.

For the rest of the half both defences held. I stood looking dejectedly down field, the Captain's cap pulled down well against the sun, pretending not to overhear the hurtful observations of some village supporters behind the goal. When the final whistle blew I slunk hastily away.

The Captain was, if anything, more terse towards his grandson than he was to me as we gathered in the house for tea. He looked upon the afternoon's embarrassment as but one of the tests I had to take. By the time we went into dinner my litany of disaster had considerably lengthened. I went down 70-1 at snooker, was rubiconed at piquet, and overrun at Chinese chequers. Sobs was looking more wretched with every result, and I was glad when after dinner he was ordered up to bed. It spared him the sorrow of seeing me go down 3,000 points at bridge, partnering one of our dinner guests, Mrs Lomax-Hull. It was no more than the downward curve of our relationship required. We had sat next to each other at dinner and I had been unable to establish much rapport. She restricted herself to asking whether I had read various recently published books.

'No, I'm afraid I haven't,' I would say apologetically. 'Is it good?' She would then say that she hadn't read it either, but she'd heard good things about it. When she put the fifth such proposition, about a biography of Cézanne, I thought myself on safe ground and said that indeed I had read it, and thought the relationship with Emile Zola had been poorly handled. At this she looked surprised, and said, politely, that most of the informed opinion tended to be against me. She then instanced several things about the book that hinted that she might indeed have read it. Which certainly I hadn't. We were now in an irreversible cycle and by the end of the evening her exasperation with me was beginning to strain her manners. She paid up and went home with only fairly good grace, stopping at the door to suggest that I might do better to stick to football.

What was certain was that I should do better to stick to fishing. Sobs asked me at breakfast how I'd got on at bridge. Since the Captain was at the table, I had to divulge the truth. Sobs appeared dejected and looked towards his grandfather in the hope that there might have been some mitigating circumstances. There weren't.

'Are we fishing today?' he asked the Captain.

'Yes, I think so.'

'I bet Mr Hartley wins this one.'

There was such despondent appeal in his voice that I knew I had indeed to win. It isn't a phrase, applied to fishing, of which I much approve; but if catching fish is the yardstick of angling skill, it is a phrase I readily understand. And on that occasion I resolved to win – for Sobs, for Combermere, and for myself. Not necessarily in that order.

'I bet Mr Hartley catches Moby,' Sobs said.

'You'd never catch Moby on a fly,' the Captain said.

'Who's Moby?' I asked, though I guessed it was a fish I had to catch.

They told me.

We went down to the river about half past eleven, pausing to have a word with the referee on the way, who was clearing one of the banks. He made no reference to my appearance on the football field and civilly wished me good luck. Sobs, who with the benefit of long hours of tuition was just about able to make a showing on the river, went

down to the lowest beat, the Captain was next, and I was positioned on a beat that had as its upper boundary the domain of mighty Moby.

Nothing went right. I had a reasonable grayling, which tangled me up in the weeds, than I lost my Caperer and most of my cast on an overhanging alder branch. Then I put down a brown trout with a clumsy cast and sat down to eat my sandwiches.

Thoughtfully, I tied a Greenwell's Glory, which can work nicely late in the season on a chalk stream. The river was quiet, and prospects not too encouraging. It looked as if Sobs's worst fears were going to be realised. The champion of Combermere was going to fail again. Then something dishonourable and uncontrollable possessed me. I trimmed the dressing away from my Greenwell's Glory and impaled a piece of bread crust from my sandwich on the hook. Then I walked up towards the place where mighty Moby lay, passed beyond the little bridge which was my rightful boundary, looked shiftily round to see if I was being watched, and let my cast run down with the bread.

These sort of fishing anecdotes can be prolonged indefinitely with flowery descriptions of the natural surroundings, the fisherman's innermost thoughts, the essence of the dry fly art; when what you want to know – or at least what I'm going to tell you – is that on my third run down stream Moby took the bread. I have a long experience of fishing, but I think I could say that was the most exciting moment of my fishing life.

The reason, I am sorry to admit, was because it was suffused with guilt. There was the spice of wrongdoing, which I had expected to deplore, but which completely captivated me. All pretence of sportsmanship deserted me. Like almost everybody else I was a cheat; but the prospect of Sobs's face when I produced my fish was the only light that penetrated my moral darkness. I had to catch Moby; I simply had to.

I did. I scrambled him ashore, half turned the net to hold him down and thumped him with a convenient but rotten piece of wood, which broke in half across his head. It had been a near thing; he had worked the hook clear as I got him on the bank and the last minute or so before I landed him he must have been close to freedom. He was ugly but he was huge. I looked up and down the river. I was alone.

I'd say I'd caught him on a Caperer (upstream of course), and play it down as a lucky freak, at the same time investing my account with enough incidental and arcane lore that they must conclude that quality had outed. I retrieved the smeared cast from the mesh of the landing net, hastily detached the hook and replaced it with the Caperer. My fingers were trembling, I was laughing to myself. And then, as if in some terrible moral declaration, the fish, only stunned, thrashed into life on the bank and, still entangled in the net, regained the river. The net and the quarry sank together. I could see the handle of the net about three feet under the water, protruding from some trailing weed. I leaped in after it, grabbing at it frantically, floundering up to my shoulders as the soft mud clutched at my gumboots. My hat came off and floated insolently down river until it became waterlogged, turned turtle and disappeared from view.

I retrieved the net. Moby had returned to his domain.

There was something so conclusive, and moral, about my discomfiture that I regard it to this day as my redemption. It makes me feel human that I know how it feels to be a cheat; but I am glad that on that occasion my cheating didn't work. I am not so ingenuous as to suppose that my experience is in any way synonymous with life. Too many Mobys are daily foully caught that further the good fortune of those who ill deserve it.

When I joined the others, fishless, down the bank, the Captain laughed good-humouredly and supposed that it was Moby that had dragged me in. No, I was able to say in honesty, Moby hadn't dragged me in.

The Captain had caught one grayling, Sobs had caught two smallish trout. I had nothing. In letting Sobs down again, I had this time done him proud. His mingy little face assumed the truculence of competitive success. He was not gracious to me in defeat, because he no longer needed me to be the champion of Combermere. He himself was it. No, he himself was he.

5
The Enemy

The Frenches would already have gone up to Scotland by the end of the summer term, so their son Rupert was to travel up with me on the night sleeper. I was invited to spend a week with them in the lodge they had taken near Fort William for fishing on the River Lochy. It was the usual arrangement, light instruction for the boy, whom I'd already been teaching on the Axe, and making up the party. Helen was happy for me to go on my own; she said it was work. By which she meant the Frenches and their friends.

Rupert was coming into his last year at Combermere, so I knew the parents a little. Giles French was a billbroker, which involved, as far as I could understand, walking round the City in a silk hat between the hours of ten and three and taking a modest turn on several million times my life's earnings several times a day, depending presumably on how fast he walked. It didn't sound very interesting but it sounded a fairly reliable way of funding fishing holidays. Mrs French was pleasant and smartly decked out, the boy was nice enough too – neither very bright nor very dim, with strong honey-coloured hair that had had a lot of brushing in the years before he got to Combermere, and plain honest looks. If the school outfitters had stocked boys to match the clothes list, it could well have been Rupert French they took down off the shelves.

Going north to fish always put me in a good mood; any inconveniences in the journey receded in the pleasures of arrival – the spice of anticipation in the early morning air and the evocative station sounds. Rupert was excited and blooming with liberation: I remembered from the start of my own school holidays that feeling of almost sensual adjustment, the feeling of being suddenly out of range. We had dinner in the dining car. He waited to hear what I was ordering and said that was just what he'd like too. We talked easily, the two of us together still in the relationship of school; but when his mother came to collect us in the morning I could tell that my holiday status – of something between guest and hireling – upset our more formal but easier conventions.

Mrs French was very welcoming without quite being warm. The same applied to Fort William, where we paused to shop: there was a slightly Calvinistic, Sunday-suited feel about the slate-roofed buildings, some dark grey stone, some rendered and whitewashed, rising steeply from the narrow pavements. We called in at the Rod and Gun Shop, half way down the main street, and I bought some flies and spare tackle. They managed the Town Water and several other Lochy beats in there and they could give me cautionary words that I'd be 'nae wise' to neglect some extra one or other of their wares. The salmon seemed to like their patterns not too bright. If so, they did well to home in on Fort William.

The Lochy flows south-west for nine miles from Loch Lochy, on the whole getting less attractive as it goes, and enters the sea in Loch Linnhe by Fort William. The glen through which it descends is thickly wooded, principally with deciduous trees, but though the banks are mostly tree-lined, casting from the open stony shores and gravel banks is easy. However, this is water with a will of its own – wide, deep and powerful, even in summer, and you need chest waders and a wading staff.

Our shopping done, we made a detour to see where the Caledonian Canal drops down to Loch Linnhe by a famous and spectacular ladder of locks; so it was late morning by the time we reached the lodge, a serviceable but unpretentious affair a good bit higher up the glen. A young woman with a beehive hair style and an unexpectedly grand voice came out to meet us. She was introduced to me by Mrs French as 'Diana who's doing wonders looking after everything'. I said I was sure that Mrs French was right. At this Diana gave me a low-wattage smile, looking me up and down in evident disappointment. Then a languid woman appeared, thirty-five years old or so, with a smart tweed skirt and a dark red jersey. This was Mrs Hardisty.

'Not gone fishing, Pat?' Mrs French inquired. It was a question, as I would explain to my Latin class, that presupposed the answer no.

Mrs Hardisty shook her head.

'Betty and the men went off in a squall of testosterone. I thought I'd do something a little less energetic later on.'

Rupert was looking at his mother for elucidation. Instead he was kissed by Mrs Hardisty and rather awkwardly bumped his head against her cheek. She laughed and moved across to shake hands with me. Mrs Hardisty was all right. No enemies so far.

My relationship with Eric Preston-Locke, however, seemed blighted from the start. I sensed he was trouble when I saw him coming up the path with what turned out to be Mr Hardisty. He was in his early forties, loud, *faux bonhomme*, with a sense of confidence about himself that from my kneeling position by the rod room window looked seriously misplaced.

He greeted me patronisingly, asking only if I'd been out yet with Rupert. I said that Rupert had come down to the river with me and I'd been lucky enough to catch a salmon almost at once. That was unpopular: Preston-Locke had had three consecutive blank days. Then I made matters worse by saying that the river was rather strong for a boy and that he wouldn't really be able to manage a salmon rod properly without a helping hand. Preston-Locke had bought a salmon rod for Rupert for this very holiday and was proposing to make a presentation of it during dinner. He told me this, with evident enjoyment of my acute embarrassment. I recognised an enemy. Then he stood up and said he thought he'd earned himself a drink.

When I saw his wife I was inclined to agree with him. Betty Preston-Locke was built like a branch of Woolworth's, with forearms like Popeye, only without the tattoos. Well, I assume without the tattoos. She had twice been English women's casting champion, or thereabouts, and punched a line into the wind as if she were using a twelve-bore.

She was fagged out, she told us, and she hadn't touched a fish all day. She proposed to take a short nap on the sitting-room sofa before she had a bath. She bore down on the sofa, not so much walking as appropriating the spaces in front of her in sequence, then curled and fell like an Atlantic breaker, heaving up her legs to take full occupancy. Within a matter of moments she appeared to be asleep.

This physical forthrightness was as nothing, in her husband's eyes, when set against her good connections and her private income. The Enemy was an estate agent specialising in sporting properties. He was athletic, aggressively competitive, quite a good, rather showy fisherman, and a knowall. At dinner he would lapse into bouts of innuendo with the lady cook, or saturate us with self-congratulation in the guise of anecdote. Finally, he called me 'Harters'. He was not among the Almighty's best work.

Mr Hardisty, by contrast, was rather a trump. He was quite bad at doing everything, but very good-natured, not unamusing and he went out of his way to make me feel one of the party. I couldn't be certain, watching them together, that he commanded 100 per cent loyalty from his wife. They had no children, but probably Mrs Hardisty was one of those who might make temporary departures but would ultimately fly back to a friendly perch. In which case Mr Hardisty could study the skies with a degree of confidence.

This left us with our host and hostess, crisp as new notes. They were punctiliously civil, but they weren't people to whom you felt you could be close. There was a lack of spontaneity about them, you felt they regarded cordiality merely as a social obligation. Their son they treated like an expensive toy. Which in a sense he was.

It rained hard that night. The Enemy and I were first into breakfast.

'Are you taking Rupert out?' he asked. The topic seeemd much on his mind.

'I hope so,' I said. 'We'll fish from the bank. I don't think he ought to wade. The river's quite strong.'

'Come on,' the Enemy protested, 'he's not a baby.'

'No,' I agreed, 'he's a twelve-year-old undrowned boy.'

The Enemy didn't like this. He stabbed his fried egg with his knife and watched the yolk seep over the white.

'Pathetic,' he said.

Mrs French came in, trim as trim could be. She went over to the serving table and speared a sausage.

'Are you taking Rupert out?' she asked over her shoulder.

'I hope so,' I said. 'He'd like to go, wouldn't he?'

'Yes, I'm sure he would. But with all this rain, won't it be a bit dangerous for wading?'

'We'll fish from the bank,' I said, smiling a good morning

to Mr French who'd also joined us and was peering round to check that all our needs were served.

'Good morning,' said Mr French, 'I hope you slept all right. Will you be taking Rupert out?'

'I've just asked him that, darling,' Mrs French interposed, 'and he thinks it's a bit dangerous for wading. They'll fish from the bank.'

'Oh, yes. Good,' said Mr French. 'Morning, Hardisty,' he called out as Mr Hardisty came in. 'Sleep well?'

'Logsville,' said Mr Hardisty. He peered out of the window, frowning at the raindrops coursing down the pane. 'Noah's in the money. Is Rupert going out?' Then, as Mrs Preston-Locke joined us, 'Good morning, Betty.'

'Morning,' Betty replied in her husky baritone. 'This rain should stir up the fish. Is someone taking Rupert out?'

We'd started to update her on this point when Rupert himself appeared to a chorus of 'Good mornings' and one 'Good morning, darling'.

'Could you take me out this morning?' he asked me.

There was a simultaneous jumble of affirmative replies. The Enemy's was not amongst them.

We took my thirteen-foot split-cane rod, with a silk line dressed to float, and a nine-foot cast with a breaking strain of fifteen pounds. Rupert was carrying my large landing net, which I preferred to a gaff or tailer. Our fly patterns were Blue Charm, Hairy Mary, Jeannie, Lady Caroline and March Brown, dressed on size 6 irons. I decided we should fish a single fly, conscious perhaps that I was the one who would be clearing Rupert's snags.

He kept up a patter of questions as we walked down through the woods, with water dripping all around us and an aura everywhere of damp decay. The lower branches were coated with lichen; underfoot it was like a huge mossy sponge of green and grey. We came past a startling cluster

of toadstools, some straight out of children's illustrations with bright red caps and big white blobs, some more restrainedly pernicious. Rupert stooped to pick some, then showed me the undersides, asking what I thought would happen if you ate them.

'Dreadful things, I should think. You could probably try them out on Mr Preston-Locke.'

I guessed he would interpret it as a compliment to the Enemy's manliness, but it wasn't so intended.

As we got near the river, Rupert ran ahead and stood on the bank watching it in silence. I came up to join him and he turned to me and, very simply, laughed. I knew exactly how he felt, it was a perfect expression of anticipation that fishermen everywhere would understand.

I showed him first where we would expect the fish to lie – in the shallower water in the streamier parts of the pools, to either side of the fast current at the head or tail of the pool, close to promontories, behind boulders.

'How many fish do you think there'd be in the stretch we can see?' he asked.

'No idea,' I said. 'But more than you're going to catch.'

We did some practice casts together, keeping to the bank, then we went up to the head of the pool, and I showed him where to lay his cast, with a short line to begin with, at an angle of about 45 degrees, allowing the line to swing round on the current. Without moving, we should then extend line until we were covering the full width of the pool. Then downstream a couple of paces and the mixture as before. He managed it quite well.

At about the tenth cast the line checked and Rupert ripped it backwards with a shout, quailing away as it looped back in his face. I sorted out a modest tangle and just in case it might have been a salmon that was in a fly-taking mood, I cast out into the stream and let the line come down over the same place, thinking at least that I might set my mind at rest that it had only been some underwater snag. Nothing happened. I tried once more for luck and the line checked again. I didn't strike and then I felt that heart-stopping downward pull. I struck and we had a salmon on the line. It veered away and down into some deeper, slower-running water, and kept steady for a while. I didn't dare be rough with it, for I knew there were plenty of salmon in the Lochy that would come off best in a tug of war with a breaking strain of fifteen pounds.

'This one's yours,' I called to Rupert. 'Take the rod.'

He was beside himself with excitement. I told him what to do: sometimes he did it, sometimes he didn't. For the next twenty-five minutes we scrambled up and down, often in almost resigned suspense as the fish took a firm hold and we thought it must break us. At one moment, when Rupert slipped on a rock, he dropped the rod, but I managed to retrieve it and keep in contact until he regained his footing and could take it back.

I think he would have given almost anything to carry back that salmon to the lodge. We saw it several times, it looked all of fifteen pounds. Then gradually we began to get the upper hand, until to my shouted instructions Rupert managed to ease the fish almost to where I was craning forward with the landing net. At the last moment it swayed away again just out of reach. Rupert brought it round again with a firm, even pull, and I lunged with the net. The rim came up under the fish's belly and I lifted it awkwardly part out of the water without getting it down into the mesh. It reared and thrashed away backwards, throwing its whole weight on to the taut cast. It was too much. The cast broke. I looked at Rupert in helpless, speechless apology. He burst into tears.

Not only was I supposed to be the fishing maestro, but I was an accepted part of school authority, which totally ordered Rupert's life for some three-quarters of the year. It wouldn't have come easily to him to punch me in the face, but it was probably no more than I deserved. As it was, the Combermere anti-sneaking code didn't even permit him to state specifically that I had dislodged the salmon with the landing net; he reported in the lodge only that I had let him play the fish but that 'it had got knocked off at the last minute'. The astuter detectives, however, deduced from this that I must have been the culprit. I might have said in my defence that I had actually hooked the fish and had spent twenty-five minutes supervising the playing of it, but the only thing that weighed – in the absence of the fifteen-pound fish – was that Harters had completely ruined Rupert's holiday.

My principal critic was of course the Enemy, whose exaggerated concern for Rupert was really only a device to emphasise my discomfiture. The others, as a result, went out of their way to establish their neutrality and Mr Hardisty, conciliatory philosopher that he was, said several times 'That's fishing for you.' This merely encouraged the Enemy to carry the confrontation a stage further, as Rupert got up to go to bed, by promising to take him out the following day.

I could see the boy was embarrassed at finding himself a pawn in the plans for my humiliation and he looked at me a little pleadingly as he thanked the Enemy and wished us all goodnight. As he closed the door the Enemy winked very obviously at Mrs French and asked me whether I knew the Latin for landing net.

I watched them set off after breakfast, the Enemy full of confident forecasts and advice deliberately contradictory to my own, and Rupert swishing his brand new salmon rod. Mr French, feeling perhaps that the schism between his guests reflected rather poorly on his skills as host, turned to the rest of us and laughingly observed that the Enemy could never resist a tease.

Returning in the early evening with two fine salmon, I tried not to allow myself cheap satisfaction at the news that Mrs Hardisty delivered from a deckchair outside the rod room door. Rupert had returned before lunch soaked through, not only with chattering teeth but with one less than when he'd started out. His rod was broken and his shoulder quite severely bruised. His mother had taken him to the cinema in Fort William for the afternoon.

She clapped her hands to see my fish and I forced myself to inquire whether any of the party had shared my luck.

'Not a sausage,' she said. 'Though I think Betty may have lost one.'

I went into the lodge to enjoy my commiserations with the Enemy. I should have known my man.

'Hello, Harters,' he said breezily, 'you've been teaching Rupert bad habits. Poor old chap took a horrible tumble. I think he's rather gone off fishing for the moment.'

I was about to offer some inadequate riposte when Mrs Hardisty followed me into the room with her arms extended.

'He's caught two huge fish,' she said.

The Enemy rode the blow. He knew where I'd been fishing.

'Bet you caught them in Morrissey's Pool. Or the Larch.' He made it sound as if any fool could catch fish there.

'Morrissey's,' I said.

He nodded as if to say 'I told you so.' 'Anyway,' he went on, 'I hope you're in trim for the race up Ben Nevis.'

I blinked. The man was insane. You could see Ben Nevis from the lodge. It was simply enormous.

'What race is that?' I asked eventually.

'Lodge sweepstake,' the Enemy said. 'Tomorrow.'

'But tomorrow's Sunday.'

'I know,' the Enemy agreed, 'but no one's asking you to sing "Abide with Me" at the top.'

I sat down heavily. The jigsaw was beginning to fit into place. The Enemy was committed to my physical disintegration.

The peak of Ben Nevis, seen from the Fort William side, is a squarish, bleak, mauve-grey lump lurking behind a curving green ridge. The scrub grass on its lower slopes is dotted with fallen boulders and scarred by countless rivulets and tiny streams. A rough track leaves the A82 just north-east of Fort William and leads south-eastwards up Glen Nevis, alongside the modest River Nevis, running out at the foot of the most commonly used path up the mountain. The path is a killer, starting off quite gently but soon becoming steeper, a series of rough, natural steps ranging in height from six inches to three feet, no two the same

We took the cars as far as we could. Then we all got out for the Enemy to explain the rules. It seemed the field had been whittled down to two: the Enemy and myself. I was to be allowed a fifteen-minute start and the sweepstake hinged on the time it took for the Enemy to catch me – although the option, he graciously conceded, was included of my outstripping him.

'We all put in seven pounds and one pound each for Rupert,' the Enemy explained. 'Then we put these cards' – he held up a small bundle – 'into a hat. On each card is a time – starting at twenty minutes, then at ten-minute intervals up to ninety minutes, and finally the "not caught" card. After the race we all draw cards and the one who gets the nearest to the actual time wins the sweepstake.'

I realised that the Enemy's motives in staging such a contest were simultaneously to show off his athletic skills and make me look ridiculous. It has to be said that in the latter regard I had to some extent preempted him. I was wearing a cricket shirt, plus fours and some extraordinary shoes that Helen had bought me from the Army Surplus Stores, with heavy ridged soles and rather aggressive toecaps. I think they must have been a discontinued line; a sign in the shop window said jokingly – or perhaps not jokingly – 'As dropped on Cologne', and certainly I shouldn't have wanted to be underneath them when they landed.

The Enemy pointed out the recommended route and said that Mr Hardisty had agreed to act as timekeeper. I assumed that he would know the Enemy's form, so I was unsettled to find him according me the rather apologetic support of a second who has already ordered the undertaker. The Enemy and I were both asked to synchronise our watches in case the moment of overtaking came when we were out of sight of the timekeeper, possibly in cloud. Then Mr Hardisty called out 'One, two, three, GO,' and I shot off up the path if not as fast as my legs could carry me, at least as fast as, in my Army Surplus aerial bombardment boots, I could carry my legs.

You don't need rope and suction boots to beat Ben Nevis; the route up it that had been indicated to me by the Enemy could be negotiated fairly easily by a highly trained gazelle. At the top, should the pursuit have lasted that long, there are areas of scree, which – for the uninitiated – is large-gauge grey shingle and behaves, if you're climbing up it, like a downward-moving escalator, apart from inflicting irreparable damage on your shoes.

I had, in the Yorkshire days of my youth, climbed the local peaks – Great Whernside, Buckden Pike, Pen-y-Ghent and Ingleborough – with my clergyman grandfather, who apart from being a dedicated ornithologist, had also in earlier days done some real mountain-climbing. I never exactly enjoyed it, but I do remember a considerable exhilaration in getting to the top. There was too a certain satisfaction in stopping occcasionally to survey the view, and seeing each time a steady accretion of the landscape. It looked back at you in quiet congratulation and I always thought those regular stops were somewhat akin to the stages of the Creation. You could see why God spun it out for a week.

I decided I'd try to give the Enemy a fright by covering the first few hundred yards at tremendous speed. He assumed that my physical performance was much inferior to his own, or else he wouldn't have staged the contest. But he didn't actually know that it was. And I've seen very good long-distance runners who looked as if they couldn't run the length of a cobweb brush. I'd give him a fright.

There's nothing wrong with mountains except the gradient; but the gradient's a real design fault. After three hundred yards there was a sound of anvils in my head and I was lolling like an exhausted eland.

I sank down and affected to be attending to my shoelace, deliberately not looking back in the direction of my opponent. That first burst had been a mistake. I simply couldn't go on. I was beaten already.

Did it matter? Rupert was probably the only one who actually wanted me to win, but he wouldn't be admitting it to his parents or the likes of Mrs Preston-Locke (if such a category existed). He'd be sure, however, to put the story round when he got back to Combermere. I could see the bursar's face. In public school fiction I'd be slugging it out with the school bully in Togger's Yard. The Enemy was the school bully. I stood up and lurched ahead. Above the ring of the anvils in my head a voice called out 'Good man.' It could have been Sir Henry Newbolt. Or possibly Talbot Baines Reed. It certainly wasn't the bursar.

I fixed my eye on a vantage point a good bit higher up and I began to count quite slowly up to a thousand. I found that on the short steep bits I scrambled up quite quickly and then recovered my impetus with long steady steps. In an unexpected way it was physically – and certainly psychologically – better than stopping to rest. I began to get my second wind.

I was still a couple of hundred yards short of my vantage point when I'd counted to a thousand, so I recited chunks of 'Atalanta in Calydon' as I climbed on up. Not that I had much in common with the hounds of spring, but the piece has a locomotive rhythm that comes in handy when you're running up Ben Nevis. I reached my vantage point. It was the first stage of the Creation. I turned round to survey the first stratum of my world.

On the path a good way below me the Enemy was lying face down. Three of our party – it looked like Mr French, Mr Hardisty and Mrs Preston-Locke – were hurrying up towards him from the cars.

I took my time coming down because I was afraid of what I'd find. Also, if there were repairs to be done, the others would be much better at it than I. I saw them turn him over. Blessedly he wasn't dead. They propped him up and squatted round him.

As I came up he nodded to me, with a grimace that conceded defeat. His face was a bad colour and he was sweating. 'Had a bit of a turn,' he said and held the front of his shirt. We waited with him for an uncomfortable quarter of an hour. Then he stood up, brushed aside our words of caution, and said he thought he could make it slowly to the cars. He walked between Mr French and Mr Hardisty, with an arm round their shoulders.

We got him into the back of the Frenches' car and he wound down the window. 'I'll be all right,' he kept saying, opening and closing his eyes in a not very reassuring way. Rupert, at his mother's side, looked shocked and bewildered.

'Shall we have the sweepstake,' said Mr Hardisty, 'and then we'll get back to the lodge.'

Mr Hardisty passed round the hat in silence. We each took out a folded card.

'Right,' said Mr Hardisty, 'call out your numbers. The

86

official result is 'Not caught'. I've got seventy minutes.' He looked at us each in turn.

'Forty minutes,' said Rupert.

'Eighty minutes,' said Mrs French.

'Ninety minutes,' said Mr French.

'Fifty minutes,' said Mrs Hardisty.

'Thirty minutes,' said Mrs Preston-Locke.

'Twenty minutes,' said I.

'Not caught,' said the Enemy, successful in defeat but unconsoled.

6

The Tip Off

I had a colleague at Combermere who was very pedantic on the subject of coincidence. I mentioned to him once that seven people in the last four generations of my family had died on or within three days of 23 August. I had expected that this sombre multiple accomplishment would bowl him over, but he was quite unimpressed. Did I realise, he said, that almost every day of the week I saw scores of people for the one and only time in my life? What did I suppose the odds were against seeing any one of those at any given time on any given day? Put like that, I had to agree, should Uncle Reggie keel over on 23 August next, he would – in comparative terms – be no more than fulfilling the obligations of a short-priced favourite. Which is to say that some pretty unexpected events tend to be lining up around the corner. So I suppose that on looking out of our caravan on the first morning of our fishing holiday on the Teifi I shouldn't have been surprised to see six members of the Llanfyllin Message of Hope Tabernacle Choir driving tentpegs into our field.

But I was. More than that, I thought the farmer who had let us park there for a not ungenerous consideration was slightly offside in not advising us that the songsters would be pitching their tents alongside. I voiced my reservations to

Henry Fisk, my fishing companion from university days, who was still hunched up in one of the monastic bunks of the Comfyranger. I didn't know, of course, until the secretary told me some minutes later, that the rather under-nourished-looking people I saw busying themselves with peg and mallet were the quarter-finalists of the Llandysul Regional Eisteddfod maintaining their unison with a few days under canvas.

The Teifi was Henry's idea: he said he'd heard good things about the river from an aunt who lived in the area. Neither of us had been fishing in Wales so we decided to give it a try for a few days in early September, just before the start of the Combermere Michaelmas term. Our wives condoned these fishing breaks on the understanding that they weren't excessively extravagant, so when we found we couldn't stay with Henry's aunt we hired a caravan from an advertisement in the *Western Gazette*. It was described as 'good roller, sleeps two'. We expected the rolling to be a forward impulse dictated by the wheels, but it turned out to be the lateral swinging of the coachwork that the advertiser had in mind. And though, to be fair, two of what was not specified in the phrase 'sleeps two', we felt we'd been tricked into supposing it meant two people of average size.

The Teifi rises amongst the steep hills that surround the ruins of Strata Florida Abbey in Dyfed and flows south-westwards and then westwards, down a green and fertile valley, through Tregaron, Lampeter, Llanybidder, Llan-dysul, Newcastle Emlyn, Cenarth and Lechryd to enter the sea at Cardigan. We had arranged to fish the river – for salmon – below the famous falls at Cenarth. Here the Teifi is some twenty to thirty yards wide, deep and quite power-ful, especially when there has been rain in the hills. It flows through pasture land and the banks, though wooded in places, are chiefly open.

Cenarth Falls themselves are rather spectacular, covering

a distance of perhaps a quarter of a mile. Having meandered for miles down the valley, growing on its way, the river is suddenly squeezed into a wooded gorge where it drops to Cenarth's graceful eighteenth-century bridge in a series of short dramatic waterfalls. We were told that fishing between the falls was prohibited to prevent people 'snatching' – deliberately foul-hooking – salmon and sea trout; while the water immediately below the falls was the last outpost of traditional coracle fishing in Wales. These almost circular craft, propelled by a single ash paddle, were built on an ash frame and covered with tarred hide. You wouldn't find me in one.

Spring was reputed to be the best time for fly-fishing for salmon on the Teifi, which made our choice of September a little behind the clock. But the river looked exciting and Cenarth itself was a pretty village, with two pubs and a working smithy, the grey stone of the houses relieved by brightly painted doors and shutters. We'd set up in the corner of Farmer Evans's field, just above Cenarth, after a journey of considerable anxiety. The motions of the caravan behind the car made driving more like the playing of an enormous fish, but at least so completely exhausted us that we slept like tops. I woke up about 7.30, aroused I suppose by the early arrival of our fellow campers, which after a prolonged stare through the caravan window I reported to Henry, adding a word of reproach about Farmer Evans's code of business practice.

'Go and find out who they are,' Henry said, 'while I get my things together.'

I climbed out of the caravan and walked across to the tentmakers, uncertain of whom to accost. A man in his thirties detached himself from the rest and came over to greet me.

He identified himself as the secretary of the Llanfyllin Message of Hope Tabernacle Choir. A few of them, he said, came on a camping holiday every September. He told me of the choir's favourable showing in the Llandysul Regional Eisteddfod. The phrase 'quarter-finals' was tailor-made for the singsong intonation of his voice.

'Do you sing on your holidays?' I asked a little anxiously.

He laughed. 'Not much. We go walking, looking at the countryside – that sort of thing.'

'Ah,' I said.

'You're from England?' he went on. 'The farmer didn't tell us about you.'

'No, he didn't tell us about you either. We're just two, my doctor friend and myself. We're here to fish.'

'Ah,' he said.

I went back to Henry. 'They're songsters. Message of Hope Tabernacle.'

'Oh dear,' Henry said.

I watched them slyly out of the window. They were quite smart at running up the tents, one three-songster head-quarters model, and three soloist models. After that they unloaded their vehicles, a car and a rather battered van, and then the secretary lit up a primus stove and started making breakfast.

I maintained a running commentary on these activities for Henry's benefit and passed on any significant field data – the secretary was carrying the teaspoons in his pocket, songster 4 had three sausages but appeared not to like tomatoes. An unsophisticated behavioural pattern began to develop – songster 3 threw stones at the kettle and after breakfast songsters 4, 5 and 6 played french cricket with an apple and a wooden spar torn off the farmer's gate. Henry thought these men unlikely to be true artists. He also thought they kept rather odd hours. It was quite early, after all, to be arriving on the first day of your holidays. I could see that something was making him uneasy. 'Let's make sure we're locked up,' he said.

We set off about half past eight, waving to the songsters as we walked up the field to the car. In Cenarth we stopped at The Three Horseshoes for breakfast and then, after a glance through the newspapers, we went on to fish, parking in a gateway before walking down to the river bank.

The salmon average about eight pounds on that water, with a fifteen-pounder considered a big fish. I had my thirteen-foot split cane rod, with a silk line – undressed, to encourage it to sink – and a nine-foot, twelve-pound breaking strain, nylon leader; and my big cane-rimmed landing net with a knotted mesh (I've never used a gaff – I find there's something unnecessarily crude about them). For flies, we'd been recommended patterns with a bit of orange or red in them for the autumn. I had Stoat's Tail, Garry Dog and Willie Gunn, all tied on double size 8 hooks.

The morning's fishing was pleasant but unproductive. At lunchtime we went into Cenarth and had a sandwich and a glass of beer in The Three Horseshoes, amid an indeterminate feeling that visiting anglers weren't all that welcome on the Teifi. This was before the Welsh wrecked their game fishing in the 1960s and '70s, in an anarchic and destructive phase when it was effectively uncontrolled and the salmon and sea trout stocks were seriously depleted. But even then, in the 1950s, although one couldn't take issue with the majority of the locals, there was a mood of Wales for the Welsh that made an Englishman feel that its corollary, Welsh for the Welsh, would serve them right.

The water bailiff, who came walking up the bank in mid-afternoon, was also something of a threatened species. Many of them, in the village communities, had to put up with some very rough treatment when the poaching began to get out of control, with dogs shot or poisoned, windows broken, gardens sprayed with weed-killer, vehicles damaged, wives and children taunted.

He stood and watched me as, using a single fly, I moved

up over the pool I was fishing, a pace or so after each cast, giving as much slack line as possible to allow the fly to sink as it began its journey down and across the river. When I reached the top of the pool, he called out 'Good afternoon.' It was a summons. I reeled in and came back to talk.

He was courteous but brisk. I established our local connection with Henry's aunt, which seemed to redeem my Englishness a little. He asked where we were staying and I told him about the caravan in Farmer Evans's field. Weren't there some other people, he asked, just arrived? Yes, I said, singers from Llanfyllin. He looked puzzled. What were they singing there? You may well ask, I said; with any luck, Palestrina rather than Ivor Novello. With even more luck, nothing. He shook his head. Well, he said, he'd be getting along.

We fished quite late, with no results. The evening was fine and serenely beautiful, strapping down the landscape in swathes of dark shadow. There was a feeling of closing time on the river, with just a hint of mist. We packed up by the car and compared notes on the day. I shouldn't have liked to count the number of evenings I'd stood like that with Henry, ever since those first undergraduate days on the Coln, being driven down from Oxford in our tutor's car, with war in the offing and all our impressions daubed in the strong colours of youth. Now we had the confidence of tested friendship to indulge each other's enthusiasms, to be fishing bores without boring each other; and our wives sensibly left us to it.

Henry suggested that we drive down the valley and find somewhere to have dinner. There were supposedly facilities for cooking in the caravan but we preferred not to put them to the test. So we drove until we found a fairly salubrious-looking hotel in one of the towns, with a menu framed by the front door – to invite you or to warn you, depending on how fastidious you were. But we weren't there to award rosettes and, besides, a day on the river makes you want to eat the chef, not criticise him. We had a bottle of inoffensive red wine with our meal and discussed what we might do differently to catch a fish or two tomorrow. Then we went out to the car and drove back to our field.

'Do you think they'll be singing?' Henry asked as we came back through Cenarth. 'And if so, what?'

I thought plainsong. No, he said, too pure; something emotional and Welsh. Neither of us was right.

A couple of hundred yards before the field we saw the songsters' van parked in the entrance to a farm track. Our gate was open, so we drove in and bumped over to stop beside the caravan. We could see lights in the tents. We went into the caravan and went to what passed for bed. 'I bet they're burglars,' Henry said as he put out the light.

I wished he hadn't said it. Henry was made of stronger stuff than I. I'm not suited to personal danger; I'm a dazzled rabbit when it comes to a confrontation. Henry, being a doctor, was rather good; or perhaps that's why he was a doctor. He was calm, positive and supremely sensible. I kept sitting up in my bunk and peering through a chink in the curtains towards the host of Midian no more than fifty yards away. I could imagine them laden with the sidearms of their trade. When I'd first seen them, I'd thought how slight they were. But there's a nasty difference between a weakling and a weakling with a mask and a crowbar.

It never could have been much of a night in the Comfyranger, but that one was memorably bad. I kept dozing off, then waking up with a start, imagining I heard people moving about outside. Henry, unhelpfully, seemed always to be asleep. I looked out of the window a score of times. There was nothing to be seen.

By morning there was no air of threat. The songsters were preoccupied with their breakfast ritual. The spoons in the secretary's pocket seemed not to have been augmented by a fresh night's haul. We began to believe in the Message of Hope.

As we drove slowly up the field to start our day, the secretary came and exchanged pleasantries through the open window of the car, giving us opinions on the weather prospects, wishing us good luck on the river. We turned out onto the road and headed towards Cenarth. The songsters' van was where we'd seen it the previous evening; but it was facing the other way. 'That's very odd,' Henry said.

He stopped our car beyond the van and got out. I saw him peering into the van through the passenger seat window, shielding the reflection with his hand. Then he walked quickly back to the car.

'They're a poaching gang,' he said quietly. 'All the gear's in the back. Nets, explosives, the lot.'

I quailed. 'What do we do?'

'We sneak,' Henry said. 'At least I do. You don't approve of sneaking at Combermere, do you?'

'While they're parked in the same field as we are,' I said with some feeling, 'I approve of internment without trial.'

We stopped outside The Three Horseshoes and went in to have breakfast. In the safety of our surroundings, with Henry very much in control and with a day's fishing ahead of me, I felt a great deal better. Over the fried eggs and bacon I could even get back to the niceties of hook sizes and the arguments for preferring a Garry Dog to a Willie Gunn; or whether or not you should keep a loop of line in your hand and release it before striking when a salmon takes. It's something that Henry did and I didn't. I wasn't convinced it made that much difference, in fact I think I once lost a fish because of it. But Henry's argument was that it enables the fly to slip back into the 'scissors' – the hinge of the fish's jaw – and gives you a firmer hook-hold.

'Right,' said Henry after his fourth piece of toast, 'time for the tip off.'

We went together to the telephone, looked up the number and rang a police station a little way away. Henry did the talking, in a Welsh accent – 'they'll probably take more notice of that.'

'I'm telephoning from Cenarth to report that a poaching gang is camping in a field belonging to Farmer Evans about a mile east of the village. You'll see a caravan in the bottom corner. The gang was out last night. They have explosives and are probably dangerous. Have you got that?'

'Yes,' said the voice the other end. 'Who is calling please?'

Henry put down the telephone.

'That should get them out of our way. They'll probably be moving on anyway.'

I congratulated him on his Welsh accent.

'It saves my getting involved and losing half a day's fishing talking to the police. If they move quickly they'll catch them with some evidence on them, in which case we can make a statement; or they'll frighten them off.'

We went down to the river feeling pleased with ourselves. We decided to keep the same beats as yesterday. There was very little wind and intermittent sun. Henry went on down river, out of sight, and I started covering the pools with a Stoat's Tail. About mid-morning I hooked a salmon, who kept me busy for nearly quarter of an hour although he wasn't much over six pounds. But with a blank day behind us, I wasn't going to rush him, especially as the river was running quite strong. As it turned out, it was the only touch of the day.

I'd just finished the sandwiches they'd made up for us in The Three Horseshoes and was starting to cover a new pool when I saw the water bailiff coming across the field towards me. He was accompanied by a policeman.

'Good afternoon, sir,' the policeman said, in a manner that suggested a handful of high trumps. 'Would you be the owner of the caravan parked in Farmer Evans's field?'

'I wouldn't be the owner of it for anything,' I replied, 'but we did mistakenly hire it.'

'We?' said the policeman.

'Dr Fisk and I.'

'And where would I find Dr Fisk?'

He enunciated Henry's name as if he were holding it in a pair of tongs.

'He's fishing lower down. What can I do for you?'

'You can explain for a start,' the policeman said unpleasantly, 'why your caravan contains four salmon that appear to have been damaged by explosives.'

'It doesn't,' I said.

'Then there must be something wrong with my eyes.'

'Come on,' I protested, 'the poachers must have planted the fish on us.'

'The poachers?' the policeman said in a don't-give-us-that-now sort of voice.

'The men in the tents. In the same field.'

'The only people in the field were the members of the Tabernacle Choir.'

'They're the poachers, you cretin,' I shouted at him.

The water bailiff intervened. 'They were the choir when we were talking yesterday. Don't you remember I asked what they sang and you said you hoped it was Ballymena and not Ivor Novello?'

'Palestrina,' I corrected him weakly.

'So today they've conveniently turned into poachers?' the policeman said. 'They should have stuck with Ivor Novello.'

'Look, what is all this?' I asked. I was beginning to feel very uneasy.

'We had an anonymous tip off this morning...' the policeman began.

'That was from us,' I said.

The policeman shook his head. 'No. It was a Welsh voice.'

Then he told me what Henry had told him, and how they'd been up to the field, met three members of the choir (those, presumably, who hadn't already made a getaway or gone off to sell their catch), who'd told them about us and had shown them into the caravan. And as I clearly couldn't offer any satisfactory explanation for what they'd found there and even had difficulty remembering what I'd said yesterday, would I mind accompanying him to the station.

'I'd mind very much indeed,' I said. 'You've managed to misinterpret absolutely everything.'

He looked at me with considerable dislike.

'That sort of talk doesn't help,' he said.

I suggested that Henry should be made aware of the allegations against us. The policeman, obviously eager for a left and a right, agreed with this and we went down the bank to where Henry was fishing. The policeman outlined the facts as he saw them and instructed us both to accompany him to the station. Henry merely looked amused.

'My aunt is on the local bench,' he said. 'I must ask her whether there is any recorded case locally of a police officer behaving in a more inept and gullible way.'

At this mention of an inconvenient local connection the policeman lost some of his confidence. Henry kept up the pressure. He asked whether the policeman had considered the possibility that the Message of Hope Tabernacle Choir might be hiding their incriminating evidence in our caravan. How had he got into the caravan, which we had left locked, unless the choir members had already broken into it? Had it occurred to him that the choir was an invention? And just because they were Welsh and affected to sing, why couldn't they be common criminals like lots of other Welshmen?

The policeman had now rather lost his balance. The water bailiff chimed in to help him.

'We know they were singers,' he said. 'Mr Hartley and I talked about what they sang.'

Henry looked at him scornfully and suggested that the policeman was quite capable of making himself look a moron without any hints from the water bailiff. It must have struck the water bailiff that there was some truth in this, because he withdrew a few paces; then, as he saw the policeman's position deteriorating, he said that this wasn't really any of his business and he must be getting along.

We made our point of course. But bad luck, incompetence and prejudice, blended together, are an unnerving combination. And our experience brought us up against elements of all three.

To begin with, there were seeds of our own sowing. Henry, in reporting the gang, had used a Welsh voice in the belief that it might reach more sympathetic ears. He had also made the telephone call anonymous for the excellent reason that he wanted to go fishing without being disturbed. Both these ruses were extremely unfortunate if it became important after all to identify himself as the caller. In referring to the location of the gang, he had mentioned the caravan and so unintentionally created the impression that the caravan should be the police's target. My frivolous conversation with the water bailiff was made to seem an endorsement of the authenticity of the choir. Being seen to be experienced fisherman was, in the eye of the beholder, being seen to be suspiciously knowledgeable of the ways and whereabouts of salmon. By leaving the field before the gang, principally because we couldn't be bothered to make our own breakfast in the caravan, we had allowed them time not only to pick the lock of the caravan and steal several of our possessions, but also as a malicious joke to leave behind four salmon so badly damaged as to be unsaleable. And it was on the basis of this discovery, in the caravan to which we ourselves had unwittingly directed the police, that a *prima facie* case had been established against us of poaching with explosives.

Worst of all, it was something that the police were ready to believe. We were rather snooty anglers from England, the departing poachers were *soi-disant* Welsh Tabernacle choral stars. That's no contest, if you're talking about local allegiance. It's not peculiar to Wales, it's a variation of a familiar problem all over the world.

We could have broken down the police case because we had the muscle to do so. There were obvious flaws in it; moreover Henry's aunt was the chief magistrate in the area. It would have been unthinkable for the senior authority to close ranks around the junior. But there are plenty of instances when the temptation must be strong. When no one likes the pawn and the pawn can't cause trouble, sometimes the pawn comes off the board.

As it happened, part of the gang – the secretary and two of his cronies – made the enjoyable mistake of trying to make off with the Comfyranger. They waited until the policeman had gone away to locate us and then attached the caravan to their car, thinking this a comprehensive way of stealing those of our possessions that the other members of the gang hadn't already taken away in their van.

The unreliability of the Comfyranger now for the first time worked to our advantage. The thieves had covered only six miles when the 'good roller' rolled them clean off the road and down a twenty-foot bank into a field. From there they were retrieved, bruised but not seriously broken, and the chain of police research brought us quite quickly face to face again. They declined to identify their colleagues but, as befits good choristers, prepared to face the music.

I don't know what became of the rest of the gang. Possibly they continued to blow hundreds of salmon out of the Welsh rivers. We never heard that they were caught. Nor did we recover what they stole from us. The van, whose number Henry had noted down, turned out to have been stolen, the Llanfyllin Message of Hope Tabernacle

Choir not to exist. Interestingly, the factor that upset the policeman most was that the choir was invented. That was a betrayal on sacred ground. It's my contention that the Welsh are obsessed by singing because the intonation of their speaking voices is so irritating. But they do sing like angels. If there is such a thing as a Welsh angel.

7
About Tern

'Tell you what,' Uncle Reggie began.

I am commercially inexperienced but I know that phrase. You hear it from contractors who 'just happen to be in the area' and can macadam your perfectly decent gravel, roll the dog into the drive and jam your garage doors for a price that 'hardly makes sense'. (That part's true.) So as Uncle Reggie was only a much more likeable and more up-market variation of the roaming contractor, I checked the escape hatches and waited to hear his proposition.

It was music. He was celebrating some sort of financial touch and he'd like to take us to Lough Corrib to coincide with the mayfly. He'd asked Lawrence, my brother-in-law, and Lawrence was keen if we were. 'Let me know,' he said, and rang off.

'We can't let him,' I said to Helen.

'Yes, we can,' she said.

I rang Uncle Reggie back to say we were on. I'd fix it with the headmaster for the weekend before half term. Our daughter Barbara could stay with her grandparents.

'Terrific,' said Uncle Reggie.

Corrib is a vast limestone lough, studded with islands, some tree-clad but most not much more than rocky outcrops. It stretches over thirty miles from Maam Bridge at the north-western extremity to Galway City at the south-eastern end. It is in two parts – the main lough, perhaps twenty miles long and eight miles wide, and what might be termed the 'lower lough', immediately to the north of Galway City, some ten miles long and four wide. The fishing is famous, the place, when calm, a dream. But the weather can change rapidly and dramatically: get caught in a storm and you might be in the North Sea.

Neither Lawrence, Helen nor I had been to Lough Corrib before. Uncle Reggie claimed to have fished there 'once or twice', but when we were trying to establish which was the best place to stay, I had to read out several place names from the map. Uncle Reggie was sure it began with a 'C', on the south-western shore of the lough. Then he agreed it might be Oughterard. He wrote off to book rooms.

We flew to Dublin in a Viscount. I am nervous about air travel and I consider even four engines an inadequate hedge against the dangers. But this was rather like flying breast stroke, not exhilarating but not unduly alarming, though it helped to see the Rolls-Royce symbols on the engines as the tiny ridges of the Irish Sea edged slowly under the outline of the wings.

I love going to Ireland but I don't think I could live there. I suffer from a sense of order; when things get difficult, I need there to be a shoulder to the wheel. In England we've got used to a shortage of shoulders; but in Ireland there probably isn't a wheel.

We were to stay overnight at the Shelburne Hotel. 'Start as you mean to go on,' Uncle Reggie kept saying expansively at lunch, clicking his fingers for the waiters. Afterwards he set out for the shops and was away about an hour before returning with twelve silk shirts fom Tyson's, a quantity of slightly unnecessary fishing tackle and a stuffed

Caspian tern in a glass case. I have no idea what sort of price he paid for the bird nor what sort of shopkeeper has the optimism to hold that sort of stock; but Uncle Reggie was delighted and made me accompany him to the public library to find out from the *Handbook of British Birds* a little more about the species. This necessitated taking the creature with us and there was some doubt at the door whether the rules of the library were being breached by allowing it admittance. But we explained that it was too static to constitute a pet and we needed to bring it in to check its appearance against the reference books. The staff saw the validity of this and one of them kindly helped us in our researches, agreeing with us that its size and handsome red bill made it a Caspian tern beyond dispute.

Uncle Reggie was cockahoop, as we set off back to the hotel, that the *Handbook* conceded less than forty United Kingdom sightings. 'It's the bargain of the century,' he said. 'I bet that shopkeeper thought it was a seagull.'

At risk of being a wet blanket I had to point out that, though a live United Kingdom sighting would be an ornithological bullseye, a dead specimen might have come from anywhere. The Caspian tern is an almost cosmopolitan species. Uncle Reggie fell silent at this and it was only when we were approaching the Shelburne, along St Stephen's Green, that he popped up in his historical nugget mood with a little sweetmeat about the East India Company's early attitude to buggery at sea.

'Both of them over the side,' he said. 'No messing about.'

'Well, no more messing about,' I agreed.

'Bit rough though, isn't it?'

Yes, I said, it didn't seem very broad-minded.

Lawrence was talking racing to the hall porter when we came in. Uncle Reggie went across to join them and set the Caspian tern down on the desk.

'He's a good-looking fellow,' the hall porter said. 'Is he lucky?'

'Lucky?' echoed Uncle Reggie. 'This is the bookmakers' death, this is the counter-albatross.'

'Would he have a view on tomorrow's card at Epsom?'

'If, while we go to dinner at Jammet's, you hear a deep, loud and raucous "kaah, kaah" or a repeated monosyllable like "kuk-kuk-kuk", go for mixed trebles the favourites and count me in to a tenner.'

'You come down here, my beauty,' the porter said, and put the glass case underneath the desk.

When we came back from Jammet's, where Uncle Reggie broke the back off his chair, the hall porter reported that the bird had remained completely silent and no betting transactions had been made.

'Could have saved us a few quid,' Uncle Reggie said, taking the glass case from the porter and carrying it up the stairs.

In the morning, when we loaded our hired car, the bird was assigned the centre of the back seat, flanked by Lawrence and Uncle Reggie's rods and suitcase on one side and by Uncle Reggie on the other. I was deputed to drive. Helen sat next to me.

It's a fair way to Galway and I had a nasty feeling that Uncle Reggie might give us a bad time on the history front. As we went over O'Connell Bridge, he told us about an acquaintance of his who had jumped a horse over the parapet into the Liffey. I didn't quite know what we were supposed to make of that, but Helen said severely that she thought it was both cruel and ridiculous. Then we had a snippet about the Liberator's mother, and then the age of the oldest cow in Scotland. Then there was a prolonged silence and, glancing in my driving mirror, I was pleased to see that Uncle Reggie's eyes were closed.

The Oughterard hotel was functional, without frills. The

proprietor had wanted to be a jockey but always had trouble with the weight. There's something particularly unfair about a noticeably small man who's too big to do the only thing he wants.

'Wilkes,' said Uncle Reggie. 'One double, two singles.'

The proprietor opened a folder from which he took a letter in Uncle Reggie's handwriting. He looked at it for a moment, as if to refresh his memory, and then confirmed that he was expecting us.

'Major and Mrs Hartley,' he said, 'Room 10; Mr Wilkes, Room 14; Colonel Wilkes, Room 12.'

We looked at Uncle Reggie with expressions of silent but critical inquiry. We were familiar with his military background. He had spent the entire war in Northallerton as a second lieutenant.

He waited until the proprietor left Reception to see about our luggage.

'In countries with a turbulent history,' he said, 'travel as an oak, not a reed.'

The proprietor came back into the hotel to say there was a bird on the back seat of our car.

'It's the Colonel's,' I said. 'Just put it under the desk.'

The proprietor then told us that he'd been in touch with two gillies on our behalf, Pat and Seamus. They'd both be over at Sweeney's in the early evening, but if we didn't make contact with them there they'd be over at half past nine in the morning. Uncle Reggie thought in that case we might go over to Sweeney's for dinner and make our mark with Pat and Seamus.

Sweeney's was a wonderful, rambling fisherman's haunt just north of the town. The day's catch was laid out on platters in the stone-flagged hallway, the bar was filled with genial chatter, the visitors and the locals immediately distinguishable. Pat and Seamus were a charming pair, wise and weather-beaten, and told us what was what with such natural courtesy that we felt we were merely being reminded of things we already knew. We checked on tactics, heard how everybody else had been getting on, listened to their predictions on the weather, gave them each a bottle of whisky, and said we'd see them again in the morning. Punctiliously, they addressed Uncle Reggie throughout as 'Colonel' and myself as 'Major'.

Dinner was lengthy and congenial. Uncle Reggie involved us with a cheery inebriate called Rory, who tried to persuade us to go to a local dance. Lawrence, Helen and I made our excuses, but Uncle Reggie thought he should 'show the flag' – although anything that the Irish partygoers would less like to be shown, except perhaps Uncle Reggie himself, didn't come easily to mind. I tried to make this point to him but he had edged over the boundaries of clear evaluation; so we left him in Rory's questionable care and, across the road from Sweeney's, stood for a while in the darkness watching the glimmering power of the river fall, where later in the season the salmon and sea trout leap in prolific numbers. Then we went back to our hotel. The proprietor was preparing to lock up even as we arrived, and was not over-accommodating when we mentioned that the Colonel might be a little late.

He was. But the village dance had had a simplifying effect on his approach to obstacles and he managed to gain access to the hotel via the dining-room window. At Reception he found a light on, but no sign of life. More seriously, he had no recollection of his room number.

He extricated the Caspian tern and his suitcase from below the desk and made his way upstairs to locate an empty bed. He carried the suitcase in his left hand and the glass case under his left arm. His method was to open the door, ease cautiously forward and with his free hand feel if the bed was occupied. This involved massaging a few faces, but Uncle Reggie pulled out quickly enough to leave most of the guests wondering only if they'd had a curious dream. Being up on the second floor we were spared his investigations; because on the first landing he finally came across an empty bed. He set down the Caspian tern and his suitcase, eased off his shoes, lay down and fell almost immediately asleep.

While it was true that he was in an empty bed, it was not true that he was in an empty room. In a second bed alongside him, under the sedation of her nightly sleeping draught, the proprietor's mother lay unaware of the invasion of her privacy by Uncle Reggie and his Caspian tern. And so it was not until half past six the following morning that the hotel was riven by her cries of alarm.

I must have missed the opening exchanges between Uncle Reggie and the proprietor. When I joined the group of people on the first-floor landing, the conversational focus was on the glass case Uncle Reggie was holding rather protectively against his chest.

'It's not a seagull,' I heard Uncle Reggie saying, 'it's a Caspian tern. It was given to me by Cardinal Ronan and it's believed to have special powers.'

'Well it shouldn't be giving people a fright,' the proprietor said. Then he suggested that everybody went back to bed. The Colonel's room was No. 12. It was opposite ours.

Uncle Reggie installed himself and closed the door. The hotel settled down again. But only for a while. I heard someone come up the stairs at a run and hammer at Uncle Reggie's door. It was the proprietor. Bad reports were coming through from the dining room, where they were laying for breakfast. There was extensive damage to one window and a massive catastrophe involving the sideboard.

'Colonel Wilkes,' the proprietor called through Uncle Reggie's door, 'I must ask you to leave. You've damaged the dining room.'

Helen pulled the sheet over her head. I put on my dressing

gown and half opened our door. Opposite, I saw the proprietor was standing with his back towards me with his face almost touching Uncle Reggie's door. His clenched hand was raised above his shoulder in the just-about-to-knock position. Uncle Reggie opened up.

'We'll take care of that at 9.15,' he said. 'And if you speak to me like that again, your mother will fall downstairs and the hotel will burn to the ground. Cardinal Ronan didn't give me the Caspian tern for nothing.'

These preposterous statements, evenly delivered, threw the proprietor back onto the defensive.

'You don't expect me to believe that rubbish?' he said.

'My expectations of you just at the moment are so low,' Uncle Reggie replied, 'that I think the answer is probably yes. You should also remember that if I leave, my friends leave; and Major Hartley is not only a man with a very dangerous temper but he's also an expert on explosives. I'll discuss it at 9.15.'

Uncle Reggie closed his door. I did the same. I heard the proprietor going down the stairs.

Looking round the dining room at breakfast I could see the proprietor had cause for complaint. Reconstructing Uncle Reggie's entry was not too difficult. It seemed to have been effected in three phases. The first phase involved breaking both panes of glass in one of the windows and quite severely damaging the frame. The second phase was alighting on a table top which had not been strong enough to withstand his weight. The third phase, leading naturally from the second, was his involuntary deployment sideways on to the sideboard, which was loaded with glasses, jugs, decanters, bottles of wine and a range of other items unequal to the impact of a falling body.

It struck me as remarkable that no one had come downstairs to investigate, because Uncle Reggie's arrival in the still of night must have been extraordinarily audible. But perhaps the proprietor was either very sound asleep or out of earshot and the guests, if they heard and were surprised by it, assumed it was someone else's problem.

Uncle Reggie seemed quite unruffled. He expressed his satisfaction that none of the favourites had won at Epsom and that the Caspian tern had been prescient in its advice to the hall porter at the Shelburne. At 9.11 he left the dining-room table and went up to his room. At 9.15 he went over to Reception and set the glass case down on the desk.

The proprietor looked uneasy.

'I don't wish to threaten you with this bird,' Uncle Reggie began. 'I've no wish for your mother to fall down the stairs, and no wish for your hotel to burn down – at least during the period of our stay. If you care to ring up the hall porter of the Shelburne Hotel in Dublin he will confirm to you that the bird prevented our supporting the favourites at Epsom yesterday afternoon, none of which won.'

This impressed the proprietor. He shifted from foot to foot. 'So?'

'We are going to take advantage of its special powers. I am prepared to stake on your behalf five pounds mixed trebles the favourites at Nottingham this afternoon with a five pound accumulator thrown in for good will. You will keep the winnings and the subject of the damage in the dining room will not be mentioned again. You should anyway have been there to let me in through the front door. I could have been severely injured.'

'But,' the proprietor began.

Uncle Reggie stopped him. 'No buts. Think of your mother. Think of the hotel. This evening I shall return with a basket of brown trout from Lough Corrib and we shall find that the favourites at Nottingham have had a field day.'

'Would you pay me the stake money instead?' the proprietor asked.

'Yes,' Uncle Reggie said. 'That would be fifty-five pounds.'

'But there's forty pounds' worth of drink been lost, let alone the window and the table and all the glass.'

'Take your pick,' Uncle Reggie said, unyielding.

The proprietor thought for a while and said he'd risk the bet. But the stupid bird had better know what it was doing.

'Careful,' warned Uncle Reggie.

We were going dapping the mayfly. I had a fourteen-foot cane rod with a centre-pin reel loaded with 10lb nylon monofilament. You tied four or five feet of dapping floss – very light, multi-strand line – to the end of the monofilament, with a five-foot leader of 6lb monofilament attached to the tip of the floss, with the hook or dapping fly tied to the end of it. The trick was to drift broadside into the wind (you must have a breeze for dapping), allowing the dapping floss to carry the fly out over the water ahead of the boat. You kept the fly just tripping along on the ripple, neither drowning it nor allowing it to wave about in the air.

The gillies were invaluable. The shallow areas of all those west coast limestone loughs – the actual shores and the areas round the islands – can be treacherous, with boulders just below the surface. Lawrence and Uncle Reggie went with Pat, Helen and I with Seamus, in clinker-built rowing boats about eighteen feet long which the gillies controlled with consummate skill. No doubt these days they have an outboard motor, but this was the 1950s and there was still the feeling then that such innovations would disturb the fish.

Seamus made a strong impression on me. In a life spent close to Nature, your knowledge is more or less your experience; so that men like Seamus have powers of anticipation which to the townsman seem uncanny. He was almost infallible about where we might find a fish, the stretches not worth bothering with, what the weather would do after lunch, and when the trout would lose interest in the mayfly for the day. He was a master of his trade, a man who deserved to feel totally fulfilled. As a companion, too, he was impeccable, always knowing when to make himself useful yet never obtruding, closing behind our enjoyment like a heavy well-fitted door. He corrected our mistakes by appearing to make suggestions, in the gentlest way. At her first rise Helen struck too quickly. 'When you see him come at you,' Seamus said, 'sing most of a verse of "The Mountains of Mourne" while you watch the whole of the leader go under; then strike, and you'll have him.' It was simple, graphic and true.

The hatches of mayfly on Lough Corrib begin around eleven o'clock in the morning and continue throughout the afternoon. The fly itself is a heavyweight – a full inch from nose to tail – with a dull creamy-grey body and leaden wings. Pat and Seamus had arrived with a good supply, caught by local schoolchildren and stored in ingenious ventilated boxes. You mounted them, usually in pairs, either on specially designed hooks with fine wire spring clips on them, or simply by spearing them in a barbarous way through their thoraces with ordinary, size 8 or 10, fine wire hooks. Otherwise you could dap with a big fluffy artificial tied on a size 10 long-shank hook.

Once during the morning we came within what Uncle Reggie imagined must be shouting distance. We could just hear him bellowing something, but we couldn't make out what it was. Seamus, controlling us at the oars, caught my eye with a look of sympathetic amusement.

'The Colonel has an excitement,' Seamus said.

'Yes,' I said, 'the Colonel often has.' Just for now I preferred to be out of Uncle Reggie's range. I knew that this evening he'd have experiences to relate that would make our day look flat. He'd have caught the basket of trout he

promised the proprietor. There was even an inevitability about the success of the favourites at Nottingham. Fate seemed always to be on Uncle Reggie's side. Perhaps because he made it look to have a sense of humour.

We had lunch on an island, a picnic basket supplied by the hotel. Seamus made a fire and boiled a kettle that was obviously as integral a part of the boat's equipment as the Danforth anchor with its rope and chain. His movements were unhurried, as measured as his speech, nothing wasted. As we sat there eating our sandwiches in the sun, we got him to talk a little about himself. He had two boys, he said, one might stay, the other would go somewhere more exciting. 'I like it here,' he said, 'but it's not easy.'

I could imagine that, a life dictated by tourists, weather and the parish priest; welcoming, beautiful country but not too many perks.

'The boys get impatient,' Seamus said. 'It's too slow for the elder one. And it's life with a low ceiling.'

'It's the floor that matters,' Helen said.

Seamus smiled, pleased and a little touched.

The Lough Corrib brown trout aren't all huge – one and a half to two pounds is the norm, with a three- or four-pounder remarkable. But there's something special about the fishing: the rises can be spectacular when you're dapping, the fish coming up from great depths and swirling at the fly. And the place itself is compelling in its sheer scale, not dramatic like the lochs on Skye where Helen and I had fished on our honeymoon, but with an easy-going Irishness about the surrounding landscape, profligate green rising to heather-clad hills.

We caught fish steadily throughout the day, the morning better than the afternoon, when the breeze began to drop. Twice I had the feeling, which I have talked about to other anglers and they have had it too, of a sudden anticipation of catching a fish so strong that it amounts to certainty. I suppose it's partly the harmony of effective presentation when everything else is auspicious, so that a take seems in that moment to be the only feasible conclusion. But it's not quite as simple as that, it's more like a shaft of intuition. It must, logically, be an illusion; possibly, too, you tend to remember it when it works and forget it when it doesn't. But, for all that, it's a curious experience.

Seamus rowed us back at the end of the afternoon, with unhurried even strokes. We sat in silence, lulled by the soft slap of the water, eyes half closed, faces pressed into the sun. As we nudged against the landing stage Seamus was up to hold us steady, with a hand for Helen as she scrambled out and took the rods and fishing bags I passed up from the boat.

'It should be much the same tomorrow,' Seamus said.

We thanked him, gathered up our things and walked up towards the car. Lawrence was sitting in the front, reading. Uncle Reggie was stretched back across the bonnet, eyes closed, head on arms. He jerked up as he heard us coming.

'Didn't think much of the lunch,' he said.

'The fishing was better,' I had to agree. 'But as you'd destroyed most of the hotel, perhaps their heart wasn't in it.'

'I think their heart was in it,' Uncle Reggie countered. 'That's what was wrong.'

'Uncle Reggie,' Helen said, 'we've had a dream of a day and all you can do is complain about the sandwiches.'

'Perfection has no blemishes,' Uncle Reggie replied. Now, he said, we must go back through Galway and get the Nottingham results.

We stopped opposite a paper shop and watched him go inside. He came out with the paper and stood on the pavement looking at it. We saw him turn it on its side and study the stop press. Then he threw back his head and began to roar with laughter.

The favourites had all won of course. Uncle Reggie returned to our hotel to share his elation with the proprietor. He persuaded him to share the proceeds of the accumulator and he presented him with the Caspian tern, advising him to not abuse its special powers.

8

Hartley's Fancy

In the good old days of classical mythology, being changed by the gods into a bird or a tree simply for being inconvenient was always on the cards. I used to say that it was lucky for the bursar that I wasn't Zeus. But it was equally lucky that Zeus wasn't Zeus one night on the Torridge when I was inadvertently involved in a case of Venus Observed; or I might even now be working out my time somewhere as a greater spotted woodpecker.

The Torridge, after rising not far from Bude, runs southeast towards Dartmoor, then eastwards to its junction with the Okement, and then northwards to its estuary at Appledore in Bideford Bay. It is a typical West Country spate river, rising and falling in direct response to rainfall and drought, whisky-coloured when low, dark and dirty when swollen. The banks tend to be quite steep.

Above its junction with the Okement it is nowhere more than fifteen or twenty feet wide, and consists of a succession of dark pools joined by shallow, rippling stickles. Below the junction it becomes wider and more powerful, eventually slowing and deepening as it nears the coast. Most of the water can be waded with care, but some pools are as much as six or eight feet deep.

Henry Fisk and I had slipped off for a weekend after the sea trout. It was late July and, on Henry's recommendation, we'd booked in for Saturday and Sunday night at the Half Moon Inn at Sheepwash. We could expect good runs of sea trout, chiefly 'school peal', fish of about three-quarters of a pound returning to the river to spawn for the first time, but you could get the occasional three- or four-pounder – exceptionally, even larger.

If conditions were right, this was marvellous night fishing. You needed a moonless night or thick cloud cover, because only very rarely do you catch sea trout when the moon is shining on the water. The Saturday evening was rather muggy with cloud a good deal of the time, and quite warm. There were other anglers staying at the Half Moon and we all gathered in the stone-flagged bar before dinner to compare notes. I think it must have been almost the first time that I used the then new-fangled plastic, double-tapered floating line that came in in the mid-1950s, much more convenient than the old silk lines which you had to grease before use and dry out afterwards. I had a nine-foot split-cane rod, with my faithful old Hardy Perfect reel, and proposed to fish a single fly – ringing the changes with an Alexandra, Black and Teal, Claret Jay, and Fiery Brown, on size 10 hooks.

We dined well, with a glass of port each afterwards to put a bloom on the prospects. And then we were off into the darkness, a quarter of a mile down the winding road to the stone bridge across the Torridge. Above us, the river flowed through pastureland in a series of pools and stickles; for half a mile downstream it ran through a series of rocky pools overhung by trees, before slowing into a less dramatic stretch. I started just below the bridge, Henry went on down below me.

The river was still quite full from storms at the beginning of the week, but had settled and was fishing well. I began casting across the first pool, allowing the current to bring the fly round. The school peal were everywhere, I had two in my first five casts – strong, solid takes with the fish careering about the pool and jumping clear of the water. Then I had a rather better fish from a run under the far bank. I could hardly have wished for a more vigorous start.

On that same Saturday evening, about six miles away from where Henry and I were fishing the Torridge, Colonel and Mrs Mentmore Beenham were giving a dance for their daughter Portia, whose broad prow was taking to the social high seas. She was good with a horse, not very accomplished with her lessons, but a solid sort who would make a solid wife for the other solid sorts who all but solidified the English shires. Her father had grumbled a little at the expense of the dance and thought the young men and women who attended such occasions sounded rather rowdy. But Mrs Beenham rebuked him for being a pompous old skinflint, Portia urged him to be a sport, and mother and daughter eventually chiselled the funds out of the Colonel's bank account at Cox and King's. A small band was hired, led by a man who had played with Carroll Gibbons at the Savoy before the war and must have seen as much cheek to cheek romance along the sights of his instrument as anyone in the business. This touched a chord with the Colonel. Though hardly a Fred Astaire, he'd taken a few turns around the dance floor at the Savoy in his courting days with Mrs Beenham and thought there was nothing to beat the old tunes.

Portia meanwhile was allowed to choose the guests for her own house party and then the local squires were approached by Mrs Beenham to ask whether they'd kindly have people to stay. In several instances this proposition became a matter of weighing up whether it was worth forgoing the yearly invitation to shoot with Colonel Beenham by refusing to have unknown young men being sick in the hall.

Everard Prosser-Mann was one young man who was liable to be a problem to his hosts, a joker in any billeting officer's pack. He it was who had put up a colossal black at Pansy Vertue's junket at the Dorchester by saying goodbye to his hostess with two stolen bottles of champagne stuffed up his trouser legs. When she questioned him on the awkwardness of his gait he explained that he was Pegleg Pete the Pirate and made her a very improper suggestion, for which he was punched hard in the face by her husband. He was not one to have roaming the Aubusson, but for all that was much in demand among the young ladies of the Season. So that Portia Beenham, who was a little on the fringe of high-society events, a sort of country member as it were, was pleased that of several rival debutante attractions that weekend Everard Prosser-Mann had opted for her own.

He was slotted in with a couple who were out of touch with London life and lived in an agreeable house not far from Sheepwash. Their name escapes me, but their role in this story was merely as the destination of the young people returning from the Beenhams' dance who unwisely stopped to bathe.

It must have been after one o'clock in the morning and I was still pursuing the school peal down below the bridge. The cloud had lifted, allowing some moonlight which improved the visibility but made the fish shy. Up on the road I saw a sports car stop near the bridge and heard people getting out, laughter, girls' voices. I shrank back behind a tree as, to my dismay, three girls clambered down towards the bank and began to remove their clothes. These were long party dresses, and the girls sounded a little shrill and perhaps a little tipsy too, so the period of disrobing was extended. I was concealed from their view, no more than

thirty yards away, my eyes, making allowance for the stalks on which they were protruding, just less than that. Then, with a great shindy, the Naiads plunged, Miss Lawson, Miss Eagleton, Miss Lefevre, Venus in triplicate, unsuspecting but furtively observed.

A man in evening dress, apparently the driver of the car, had followed the girls down. He stood there urging them to be careful but showed no inclination to bathe himself. The school peal must have been surprised enough already to find these immodest dolphinettes among them and I had already said goodnight to any fishing prospects for this and the adjoining pools.

At first the young ladies splashed water over one another, then they began to swim about. The pool was not large, and they were quite near me. Having decided on my policy of concealment, I had to stick with it or be exposed as a voyeur. I pressed myself against my protecting tree.

The driver of the car – it was Everard Prosser-Mann – now called in a loud voice that he was going home and turned away as if to carry out his threat. The girls called to him to wait, and two of them started to scramble, giggling, to the bank. The third girl, in deeper water which was running quite strongly, was struggling to regain her feet. Suddenly she shouted in alarm and slipped out of sight beneath the surface.

I knew the dangers of losing your footing in a river like this. Once on the Annan I had stumbled into a hole, lost my balance and my rod, and been carried downstream, unable to right myself on the slippery rocks. It seemed absurd, having waded in quite formidable rivers, that this should be my undoing; but it seriously crossed my mind that I might drown. My struggling only made things worse and I was lucky to get lodged against a rock which, though it left me with a nasty bruise, at least checked my floundering progress down river.

Now I felt I might be witness to a wasteful accident which I had done nothing to prevent. I dithered, not wishing to reveal myself when the girls had revealed themselves too much, and not confident, even if I did, that I was tailored for the role of lifesaver.

The other girls, hearing their friend's cry for help, shrilled hysterically for the driver, who – poorly though Lady Vertue must have thought of him at the Dorchester – emerged in this moment of crisis as a hero. He threw off his jacket, pulled off his shoes, and crashed into the river towards the place where Miss Lawson (for it was she) had disappeared. Miss Eagleton and Miss Lefevre, on the bank now, with arms folded inadequately across their nakedness, moaned and shivered in a state of shocked alarm. I decided I must go in search of Henry, and while they were distracted, I slipped from my cover and ran off down the bank.

He must have been about four hundred yards below me. He heard my shouting and came running up towards me. I told him as much as I knew. Whether Prosser-Mann had managed to locate the girl and, more important, save her, we would soon discover.

He had. Miss Eagleton and Miss Lefevre had hastily reattired themselves and were stooped over their fallen comrade, preparing to help Prosser-Mann carry her back to the car, when Henry and I came galloping up in support. The rescuee looked more than a little battered, pale as a ghost, and sartorially informal in Prosser-Mann's jacket put on back to front. Prosser-Mann, drenched to his red braces, was blowing exaggeratedly hard, shaking his head and saying 'Whew', as he ran his fingers through his hair. None of the party seemed in any way surprised at our appearance, but all were obviously relieved when Henry identified himself as a doctor. They waited in silence as he examined her.

'She's got a bump on the head and she's shocked,' Henry said. 'Let's get her back to the Half Moon.'

Henry and Prosser-Mann lifted her up, the girls and I scurried behind. 'Is she going to be all right?' Miss Eagleton asked.

'Yes, I'm sure she is,' I said, though it was no thanks to me.

My role in the drama now became increasingly like Dr Watson to Henry's Holmes, bobbing around the fringe of the action with what I hoped were helpful observations. The landlord appeared and gamely poured out a glass of whisky for Prosser-Mann; Miss Eagleton asked several more times whether Miss Lawson was going to be all right and Miss Lefevre began to cry. By 1.30 the situation was pronounced under control. Miss Lawson, pale, blonde and restfully beautiful, was lying back in my bed, wearing my pyjamas, with a fetching bandage swathed around her temples.

Prosser-Mann, Miss Eagleton and Miss Lefevre set off in Prosser-Mann's car for their hosts nearby, Henry went to bed, and I made myself as comfortable as I could under a rug in the bar.

The image of the battered Miss Lawson upstairs in my bed reproached and rather unsettled me. What if she had drowned? My failure to go to her rescue hadn't been entirely prim hesitancy, it was the fear that I'd get into difficulties myself. It wasn't, however I looked at it, very gallant. So, as the light came up and before the house stirred, I got out my fly-tying kit and I tied Miss Lawson a fly, to a size 10 hook. The tying silk was black, the tail black cock's hackle fibres, the body silver tinsel ribbed with fine silver wire, the hackle mixed black and yellow cock's hackle, the wing teal. I called it Hartley's Fancy – pointedly perhaps – and in the morning, after her young friends arrived, I went upstairs to her room, my room, and gave it to her.

I stayed a brief while in rather self-conscious and inconsequential conversation, and was just leaving when Colonel Beenham put in an appearance. He found Prosser-Mann, matured into the full hero now, lying back in a chair beside Miss Lawson's bed with his legs outstretched on it, with Miss Eagleton and Miss Lefevre perched on either side. I crossed the corridor to Henry's room and stood in the doorway listening.

'So you're the hero,' Colonel Beenham was enthusing to Prosser-Mann.

'Oh, I wouldn't say that, sir,' Prosser-Mann countered.

Miss Lawson said it was sweet of the Colonel to come, and it had been a wonderful, wonderful party and Portia must have been absolutely thrilled and she was terribly sorry she'd been such a goose and messed things up.

'Nonsense,' the Colonel said. As long as she was all right, that was all that mattered.

'Do look at this,' I heard Miss Lawson say, and I guessed she was showing him Hartley's Fancy, since she went on to explain that the sweet man who was the fishing friend of the doctor and who let her have his room had specially made it for her. Didn't the Colonel think it was the sweetest thing he'd ever heard? She thought she'd have it made into a brooch.

The Colonel was not good on emotions but he looked at it with a connoisseur's eye and pronounced quite favourably on its potential with the school peal. He thought her father would be interested too – he knew Lawson was a keen fisherman. Yes, Miss Lawson, said, of course – didn't the Colonel and Daddy once fish together up on the Naver? That's right, said the Colonel, that's right. Yes, he'd be interested in that fly. What was it called again?

'Hartley's Fancy,' Miss Lawson said.

'Yes,' said the Colonel, 'Hartley's Fancy.'

Prosser-Mann, now that fishing had been covered, was the next in line for approval.

'A bit of a star swimmer?' the Colonel wondered.

'Not really, sir,' Prosser-Mann said modestly, though Miss Lefevre and Miss Eagleton claimed more on his behalf.

The Colonel thought it was a cracking good effort. Couldn't be losing nice-looking girls in the Torridge.

Miss Lawson looked contrite and said she couldn't be more sorry to have been such a bore and she just sort of slipped and luckily Everard had saved her bacon.

'Well, my dear,' the Colonel said, 'I must be getting back to the troops. Portia spoke to your mother and she's on her way. Get better quick. I like that fly. Goodbye everybody.'

'Goodbye,' everybody said. 'Lots and lots of love to Portia,' Miss Lawson added from the bed.

The Colonel tweaked his cap and backed genially out of the room and closed the door. He saw me standing in the doorway opposite and he nodded and tweaked his cap to me. Then he stumped down the stairs, humming to himself.

Miss Lawson did have Hartley's Fancy made into a brooch. What's more, she married Everard Prosser-Mann. What's even more, they sent their little boy to Combermere, though by then Miss Lawson had left Prosser-Mann for someone else (so the Vertues had their own reward for the incident at the Dorchester). The someone else she then left for someone else again. Hartley's Fancy was a catching pattern.

She came up to me at Speech Day. 'Do you remember me?' she said, and she pointed to the brooch on her lapel. It was my fly, trapped in diamonds and enamel. She was beautiful now, in that pale English rose sort of way, the girlishness gone, ceding place to a probably selfish confidence in her own allure.

'Good heavens, yes,' I said.

'Quite a little adventure, wasn't it?' she said.

'Quite a medium-sized adventure.'

She laid a hand on my arm. 'You were marvellous,' she said.

Over her shoulder I saw the bursar was watching us in resentful curiosity.

A little of Hartley's Fancy does you good.